I0494258

Home Loans for People With Bad Credit

By Ade Asefeso MCIPS MBA

Second Edition

ISBN-13: 978-1499680478

ISBN-10: 1499680473

Publisher: AA Global Sourcing Ltd
Website: http://www.aaglobalsourcing.com

Table of Contents

Disclaimer

This publication is designed to provide competent and reliable information regarding the subject matter covered. However, it is sold with the understanding that the author and publisher are not engaged in rendering professional advice. The authors and publishers specifically disclaim any liability that is incurred from the use or application of contents of this book.

If you purchased this book without a cover you should be aware that this book may have been stolen property and reported as "unsold and destroyed" to the publisher. In this case neither the author nor the publisher has received any payment for this "stripped book."

Dedication

To my family and friends who seems to have been sent here to teach me something about who I am supposed to be. They have nurtured me, challenged me, and even opposed me.... But at every juncture has taught me!

This book is dedicated to my lovely boys, Thomas, Michael and Karl. Teaching them to manage their finance will give them the lives they deserve. They have taught me more about life, presence, and energy management than anything I have done in my life.

Chapter 1: Bad Credit Repair: Defining the Problem

Before you begin the process of repairing your credit, you first need to ask yourself why you are having credit problems? Poor credit is nothing to be ashamed of. It is far more common than you may realize. Often it may not even be your fault like Mr and Mrs James.

They invested five years and all the money they saved to start a small sign company. Then one summer someone broke into their business office and stole all the computers and expensive sign-making equipment. Unfortunately they did not have any insurance to cover what was stolen, so they had to take out loans to replace the items so they could stay in business. It took them years to recover financially from that, leaving them with bad credit.

On the other hand, like Amos, some people make poor credit decisions. After Amos got his first card, shortly after graduating from University, he suddenly became flooded with offers for more credit, which he promptly took up. He wanted to show everyone that he was a success at his new career as a sales manager, so he filled up all his credit cards.

Then he began the juggling game of "robbing Peter to pay Paul," which only got him deeper in debt. He took out a consolidation loan to pay off all the cards and put the debts in one big payment, but the temptation of all the empty cards was too much for him and he filled them all back up again. He finally had to declare bankruptcy because he was so deeply in debt that it was beyond his ability to ever pay off.

So, take a good look at what is going on in your life. Why do you have credit problems? Are you in debt because of circumstances beyond your control or is it a chronic situation? Are you still getting deeper into debt or are you fixing the problem? There is no point in fixing your credit if you will just end up losing it.

If you find that you are getting too deep in debt, there are several things you can do right away to help the situation, before it gets out of your control.

1. Contact the credit card companies and see if they will work with you to help lower the monthly payments.

2. Talk to a non-profit credit counselling company, like Consumer Credit Counselling Service at http://www.cccsintl.org. They provide budget counselling, educational programs, debt management assistance and housing counselling. They have branches in many location of the United States, or in the UK talk to Citizen advisory bureau at www.citizensadvice.org.uk/ they have offices in all the major cities and town in the UK.

Beware of some "for profit" organizations that will help you with debt consolidation loans. Often they are very costly. Why go to them when you can get free reliable help from a respected non-profit organization like Consumer Credit Counselling Service?

There is no quick fix for credit problems, but with a little patience and determination, you can not only get it under control, but you can end up with great credit and the feelings of success and self-worth that go along with it. So take the first step and determine to get debt free today!

Chapter 2: Bad Credit Does Not Have to Mean Credit is Impossible

Everyone faces unavoidable financial problems at some time and find that they are in an impossible situation and unable to meet their obligations. This situation might make some feel that it is hopeless to find money help, but that is not necessarily true.

There are two types of bad credit personal loans, secured and unsecured. A homeowner may qualify for the secured personal loan and non-homeowners may apply for the unsecured bad credit personal loan. Bad credit should not affect your ability to obtain a home mortgage loan. The interest rate for a home mortgage loan will depend upon your credit rating. If the credit score is 600 or above, the borrower is usually required to pay a 5% down payment. Credit scores that fall below 580 necessitate down payments of 20% or more. However, reputable bad credit mortgage lenders do not require unreasonable down payments of 50%.

Bad credit secured personal loans are worth considering if you own property such as real estate, car, valuable jewellery, or other types of assets. However, it is important to keep in mind that the collateral may be seized and sold by the lender in the event of non-payment. In addition, there are bad credit card loans that are easy to apply for with minimal requirements to qualify, such as an income of $1,500 per month in US or £1000 in UK, proof of residency, and verifiable employment. There are reliable lenders who have reasonable interest rates and offer good financing options.

Debt consolidation loans are another option to consider if you have a history of bad debt. These loans consolidate your debts into one loan, allowing you to make one monthly payment that you can afford. Unsecured debt consolidation loans are not tied to your assets, and they eliminate annoying calls and letters from creditors, as well as helping you avoid filing bankruptcy.

Don't let a history of bad debt keep you from having the things you want or need. There are answers to your bad debt problems.

Chapter 3: How to Stop Foreclosure (Re-possession) - a Guide for Homeowners

We will use foreclosure or re-possession in this book, however they both means the same thing. One is American terminology and the other is British!

Do you know how to stop foreclosure (re-possession)? If you are one of the millions of Americans or British who are upside down on your homes and have no way out, this is a question you must ask yourself. The problem is not going to go away. If you don't answer it properly, you could lose your house and even face homelessness. For that reason, I am going to show you how to stop foreclosure.

First of all, you need to understand how we got into this situation. When real estate (property) prices were steadily going up, banks were trying to attract as many people into loans as possible. Some people wanted to buy big, nice homes. Other people wanted any home, but they had bad marks on their credit. Still others simply couldn't qualify for a home under a traditional mortgage program.

For these reasons, lenders such as Countrywide developed "creative financing" to get people into homes that they really could not afford. One of the ways they did this was to offer limited time period "interest only" or "no interest" loans. After two years, the loans re-set and the homeowner could no longer afford the mortgage.

When home prices were consistently going up, the theory was that homeowners could just refinance the mortgage. But, when the bottom fell out of the housing market, homeowners could no longer get attractive rate financing. Now, the question was how to stop foreclosure.

But the banks themselves also had to ask how to stop foreclosure. Suddenly, they were faced with a situation where assets (performing loans) were becoming liabilities (non-performing loans and bank owned homes) on their balance sheets. This caused their stock prices to plummet.

Washington and London, too, had to ask how to stop foreclosure because they were having to bail out the banks. There is even talk of nationalizing some portions of the financial sector. The federal government in the US is using the carrot and the stick approach to force banks to modify loans.

This is good news for you if you are wondering how to stop foreclosure. Now banks have every reason to work with you to keep you in your home. They are increasingly willing to talk to homeowners even before their mortgage falls delinquent.

If you have found yourself in a mortgage that got reset and can no longer afford the home, you need to talk to your lender about your options right away. There are many types of loan modifications that can help you stay in your home.

If you have a loan underwritten by Fannie Mae or Freddie Mac, the banks have to work with you under a specific set of guidelines outlined by the department of Housing and Urban Development (HUD).

There are more and more answers to the question of how to stop foreclosure. The important thing, though, is that you find the answer that is right for you as soon as possible so that you don't miss the boat and get kicked out of your home.

Chapter 4: How to Stop Foreclosure (Re-possession) Fast These Days

There are ways to stop foreclosure fast. You don't need to wait for a long, drawn out solution. Oftentimes, that only leads to you losing your home and having a bad mark on your credit. Instead, you can work with your bank or an investor to stop foreclosure fast.

The first and easiest way to stop foreclosure fast is to find an investor who is willing to pay off the existing debt on your home. Unfortunately, most investors see the glutted home market and think they can find bargains for less than the amount people owe.

That is where the short sale investor comes into the picture. He or she works with you to deal with the bank to stop foreclosure fast. A short sale is a three way deal where everyone gets something out of the bargain. The bank waives some of the principal giving the investor instant equity in the home. You walk away from a mortgage payment that you just can't make any longer. The investor gets a deal on the property. The bank gets rid of an underperforming loan. And, you get out of the foreclosure mess you're in.

A similar option is to work with the bank directly without an investor. This is called a Deed in Lieu of Foreclosure. The bank takes over the home and you walk away from the mortgage. You agree to leave the home in good shape. Too many bank owned homes have had their value seriously deteriorated because homeowners have either maliciously trashed the property or tried to sell off everything, including the copper piping, to raise money.

If you are going to agree to either a short sale or a deed in lieu, you need to make sure that the bank agrees to waive its right to pursue a deficiency judgment. If you don't do this, the bank can come after you later for the difference between the amount you owed and the amount the home was agreed upon.

Washington has given banks some incentives to help stop foreclosure fast. For instance, banks are now willing to work with people who are not yet delinquent on their loans. States are also implementing policies and laws which help homeowners stop foreclosure fast through increased bank regulation and, if the new bankruptcy reform bill passes, homeowners who pursue bankruptcy as a solution to their homeowner problems will be able to ask the Judge to modify the terms of their mortgages. Currently, Judges can do this on vacation homes, car loans, and other debts, but not on the primary mortgages.

If you do nothing, what recent history has shown us is that you will lose your home and develop terrible credit. Action is preferable to non-action. You should contact the bank immediately if you think you are in trouble with your payments and ask them what can be done to stop foreclosure fast.

Chapter 5: Bad Credit Loan: Let's Cut Through the Hype

Do you need a loan but have bad credit? Then you MUST learn a few facts your potential lender does not want you to know. If you want to avoid being "taken to the cleaners" be sure to follow the advice in this book.

Bad credit loans seem to be a hot topic these days. In fact, if you need a bad credit loan, you are likely to find an overabundance of information.

See if this sounds familiar. You need a loan. Maybe you want to buy a car, enrol in college, or take out a home improvement loan. Or perhaps you are a first time home buyer and you are looking for a mortgage. The problem is, you have got a bad credit history, and you are afraid you won't be able to find a lender.

But then you do a little research on bad credit loans and find that, there are loans for people with bad credit available! In fact, EVERYONE wants to give you a loan. Loans for cars, mortgage loans, student loans, personal loans, and loans for just about anything you want. Not only loans, but credit cards too. Why, who would have ever thought is would be so easy to get a loan when your credit history is so dismal?

So, that is great news, right? RIGHT?

Let's just stop for a moment. Ask yourself "Why is everyone so eager to extend credit to me when my credit history is so bad?"

The question can be answered in two words. Sure, you can get a bad credit loan easily enough. But you'll "pay through the nose" when it comes to the interest rate.

So "What is the 'big deal' about paying a little higher rate?" you ask. Let's look at a few figures.

Suppose you want to buy a car. After looking long and hard, you find the "perfect" car for $20,000. So you apply for a car loan and get a loan with no trouble, but because of your poor credit, you have to pay 20% interest. On a 60 month loan, your monthly payments will be $529.88.

Now if your credit were very good, you might have gotten the same 60 month loan at an interest rate as low as 10%, with monthly payments of $424.94.

The bottom line is, over the life of the loan you will have paid an additional $6,296.40 in interest that you would NOT have paid if you had gotten the loan at 10% interest. Your bad credit loan will have cost you $6,296 more FOR THE SAME CAR!

But if you think that is bad, take a look at a home mortgage loan.

Suppose you want to buy a $100,000 home and you are just thrilled to find a lender willing to give you a

30 year loan in spite of your bad credit. He will charge you 12% interest, and your monthly payment will be $1,028.61.

If your credit had not been so bad, you could have gotten the loan for a rate closer to 9%. If your credit had been very good, you might have been charged only 6% interest and your monthly payment would have been $599.55.

The bottom line; that bad credit loan will have cost you (over the 30 year term) a staggering $154,461.60 MORE than you would have paid had you gotten a loan at the 6% rate.

No, this is NOT a typo. Your lender will pocket $154,461.60 in additional interest payments because you were charged a higher rate for a bad credit loan. That's over 1 ½ times the cost of the house itself!

So why did he charge you the higher rate? Because he knows he can get it! After all, he's got you "over a barrel." He knows (and you know) that you need a loan, but because of your bad credit no one's going to give you one at a low interest rate.

Do you see now why people are so eager to lend you money in spite of your bad credit? In fact, credit reporting companies make a fortune selling lenders the names of people who have bad credit. Those lenders know they can charge them high rates, and that if they need credit, they have no choice but to pay them.

So what is the solution? You may be thinking "What choice do I have anyway? My credit is bad, I need a loan to get a house (or car, college education, or whatever) and there is just nothing I can do about it except find a lender willing to give me a loan at whatever interest rate I can get!"

But consider for a moment whether you might be looking at the situation from a completely wrong angle. Rather than resign yourself to the situation, you should be thinking about repairing your credit.

Now if you just found the house of your dreams, you may have no choice but to act now before someone else buys it. But if you can wait a couple of months, it is highly likely you can make some major improvement in your credit score and THEN look for a loan.

Maybe this is not what you wanted to hear. After all, you are looking for a loan, NOT credit repair advice. But wouldn't it be worth it to postpone getting that house or that car if it would save you thousands, tens of thousands, or maybe even $150,000.00 or more over the long haul?

If you are thinking your bad credit history is something you are just stuck with, or that it will take years to improve, you are mistaken. It's often possible to make major improvements in your credit rating in just a few months, and in some cases in as little as 30 days!

It's not that difficult either. You basically have 2

options. You can hire a "Credit Repair Agency" or you can take the "do it yourself" approach.

If you decide to hire an agency, you can easily find one in your phone book or online. Just look for "credit repair." However, it won't be cheap. Agencies usually charge from $2,500 to $5,000 or more to repair your credit. But that is still a bargain compared to how much you will be saving in the long run.

But if you think only a professional agency can fix your credit, think again! In spite of their high fees, they won't do anything for you that you can't easily do for yourself. If you can write a few letters, address, stamp, and mail them you can repair your own credit.

If you choose the "do it yourself" route (recommended) you can learn how by doing some online research. Unfortunately, along with all the good information you'll find some misinformation as well. A better option is to find an authoritative book on credit repair and follow the advice therein.

You should seriously consider postponing your search for a bad credit loan. First spend a couple of months improving your credit rating. Then you can abandon the search altogether, and begin looking for a GOOD credit loan!

Chapter 6: Home Foreclosure Listing Best Way to Find Your Dream House

A home foreclosure listing may be the best way for you to find the house of your dreams or to start building a real estate empire. You can find a home foreclosure listing on the internet. There are a variety of free sites with individual bank listings. If you are serious about finding a home in this way though, you may wish to purchase a subscription service that combines lists from all over the internet.

There are many different kinds of listings. Pre-foreclosure home foreclosure listing is one that lists homes where the homeowner is behind on their mortgage payment. While traditionally people got behind on their mortgages when they lost their job or had major medical issues, currently many homeowners are in trouble because of badly written loan agreements.

When home prices were on the rise, many mortgage brokers wrote stated income or "liar loans." These loans had introductory "teaser rates" of one or two percent. Some even included a period where the homeowner paid interest only. Of course, after a couple of years, this introductory period was up. The assumption was that at this point the homeowner would either be able to refinance and sell the home. When the real estate bubble popped, this became impossible.

As a result, there are many homeowners in pre-foreclosure desperate to find an investor who will participate in a short sell scheme to help them salvage their credit. When you get a home foreclosure listing, many of these pre-foreclosure homes will be available.

In a short sale, the investor purchases the home for less than the mortgage amount. The bank writes off the difference because it takes a bad loan off the books. The home owner walks away from a terrible situation without a foreclosure on their records. Everyone wins.

When a short sale has not been made, you get the next kind of home foreclosure listing: the foreclosure auction. When a bank is forced to foreclose on a home, after the court declares that the bank can sell the property, there is an auction which can sometimes take place on the courthouse steps. If you have a home foreclosure listing service, you will be alerted when these auctions are taking place. There is often limited competition at these auctions and you can pick up investment real estate for a song.

Often there are no qualified buyers at these auctions and the bank buys the home themselves. This presents you with the third kind of opportunity to use a home foreclosure listing: the bank owned property. When a bank owns a home, it has a number of problems. First of all, they are not in the business of renting out or selling homes at their maximum value. That means that these properties often sit unsold for a length of time. During that time, the bank must pay taxes on the property. An uninhabited home also loses value over time as people do not do the maintenance and upkeep on it. Vandals may also deface the home. If there are too many vacant homes in the neighbourhood, the value of all of the properties also decline.

For these reasons, the banks are eager to get rid of the properties they own. They generally sell the homes at a 20 percent discount from their appraised values. If you can get a home foreclosure listing of bank owned properties, you can get yourself a deal.

Having a home foreclosure listing is just one step of the process though. You need to have the education to know how to take advantage of troubled real estate and also the financing to be able to pull off the investment.

Armed with information, financing, and a home foreclosure listing, you are on your way to becoming a real estate tycoon.

Chapter 7: Bad Credit Mastercards: Build a Good Credit History

Unfortunately, many people underestimate the importance of establishing a good credit history. Because the average person cannot afford to pay cash for large purchases such as a car or home, financing has become a part of life. If you have good credit, your financing options are many. Nonetheless, those with bad credit have the opportunity to improve their credit standing, which opens the door for better financing options.

Options Available to People with Bad Credit

If you have bad credit, there are several things you can do to improve credit. For starters, it may help to rebuild or re-establish your credit history. Bad credit Mastercards can help you do this. Many circumstances justify a person needing to rebuild credit. If you have experienced a foreclosure, repossession, or bankruptcy, your credit score is likely below 600.

Low ratings make it difficult to acquire financing. Fortunately, there are several lenders that focus on bad credit. Fresh start programs include bad credit Mastercards, home loans, vehicle loans, etc. Because it is recommended that a person with bad credit obtain a credit card as the first step to improve score, you should strongly consider getting a bad credit Mastercard.

How to Build a Good Credit History?

Establishing and maintaining a good credit history is essential. Bad credit can happen very quickly. Simply refusing or being unable to pay bills on time may result in your credit score dropping significantly. While most people have good intentions, those with excessive debts usually have their hands tied.

Bad credit Mastercards offer a new beginning. If you get approved for a bad credit; credit card, avoid repeating past credit mistakes. It is realistic to raise your credit score by 100 points, or more. Building a good credit history is easy. Of course, this involves carefully monitoring your credit.

To begin, regularly check your personal credit report. Reports are viewable online. This way, if any errors or inaccuracies are present, you can easily detect them and have the matter corrected. Moreover, pay credit cards before the due date. To avoid credit problems, it will help to keep balances low, and never exceed your credit limit.

Chapter 8: The Insider Secrets of Bad Credit Debt Consolidation

What shape is your credit in? Are you floundering and finding it difficult to keep up with even your minimum monthly payments? If your credit score has dropped over the past months due to falling behind on your payments to your creditors, you may be in need of a bad credit debt consolidation plan. In simple terms, you may find that you can relieve some of your monthly payment burden by consolidating several high rate loans or credit cards into a single loan or card at a lower annual rate.

How does it work? Simply stated, you might be able to combine a number of loans or credit cards which carry a high rate into a loan or credit card that is available at a lower annual percentage. This sort of debt consolidation is often done when a consumer receives a credit card promotion offering them a rate that is lower than their existing cards, provided they transfer balances to the new card. This can be a quick and easy way to reduce the annual rate on outstanding balances and lessen the minimum monthly payments as well. However, before you combine all of those credit card balances onto a new card with a lower APR, make sure you read all of the fine print and understand exactly what you can expect to pay on the new, combined balance.

Of course, if your credit score has slipped you may find it difficult to locate a lower interest rate on a credit card. For some with bad credit debt consolidation may seem like a solution to their financial worries, but for them, finding a lender or credit card issuer who will help them lower their interest rates may seem impossible. While in the past only those with the most flawless credit could command the best rates, scanning the lending marketplace today tells us that there are lenders available for just about everyone, and even those who suffer from a very low credit score should be able to find a bad credit debt consolidation loan. Due to problems in the economy, today there are plenty of consumers who have less-than-perfect credit, and many lenders willing to service their needs.

And finally, here is a little "secret" to bad credit debt consolidation that often goes overlooked: don't forget the equity you may have in a vehicle. While most people think of equity in a home, if you have a vehicle with low miles and a low pay off balance, you may find that you can get a used car loan at a rate that is far lower than the rates you are paying on your credit cards. In some cases, these car loan rates can be had for even half the interest rate of your highest rate cards. If you are looking for a bad credit debt consolidation option, a vehicle may help you drive your way to your financial goals.

Chapter 9: Same Day Payday Loans

You can never really tell when emergencies can happen. In this kind of situation, you will need urgent cash. Certain situations like car repair, home repair, or medical attentions can give you a bad headache but through the same day payday loans, you will be able to meet your emergency requirements.

The same day payday loans can provide individuals who urgently need cash during emergency situations. This type of loan is unsecured and the lenders are at a risk. Because of this, they charge high interests. You will not need any collateral in order to benefit from the loan and it doesn't really matter if you have a high credit or low credit standing. Through the same day payday loans, you can loan amounts from £200 to £1500, depending on your monthly salary.

Once you are released a loan, you will repay it on your next pay cheque. Oftentimes, the loan terms can range from two to four weeks. Some applicants try to extend their payment terms; however, this is highly discouraged because you will only be incurring more debts on the interests.

You must be aware that the need for same day payday loans are increasing every year and because of the stringent competition in the market, lenders are now offering competitive interest charges. This is a great advantage on the part of the customers because they now have a chance to get instant money at lower rates. As mentioned earlier, individuals with low credit standings can also avail of the payday loans but they need to convince the lender about their ability to repay the loan.

The lenders of same day payday loans will also require you to provide certain documents. They have conditions before your application can be approved. To start with, you must be a full time employee. You need to provide an employment record as proof. Your income should also be not lower than £1000 per month and of course, you need to be more than 18 years old. After meeting those requirements, your loan can be approved by the lender.

Are you in urgent need of cash? Then why not check if you can meet all the requirements above? You can get the loans within a day directly in your personal bank account. If you need to pay the electricity bills, water bills, rental bills, or medical bills, same day payday loans is the best solution.

Some people only opt for payday loans after they have tried other sources of urgent cash. There are those who try to borrow money from relatives and friends. This will only work if you have not borrowed from them in the past or if you borrowed and repaid them promptly. If in case they don't have money at the moment, your option is to apply for same day payday loans.

By the way, have you ever wondered why it was called same day payday loans? Well, this is because the loans are released within 24 hours; there are even times when the loans are released less than 24 hours. You just have to fill out an application form online and then submit it for approval. Those who are constantly borrowing from the same lender have higher chances of getting higher amount of loans.

Always remember that you need to apply for the loans only when there is an urgent need for it. Visit the website below to find out more. http://www.aaglobalsourcing.com/marketplace/credit-loan

Chapter 10: Bad Credit Credit Cards Build Credit With a Major Credit Card

For the millions of consumers with bad credit and no credit, getting approved for a major credit card takes a lot of effort. Unfortunately, establishing credit is as equally challenging as re-establishing credit. Creditors consider both types of people as risky applicants. Thus, they are less eager to extend a line of credit. However, there are ways to get around this problem. Bad credit; credit cards are intended to make it easier for some to obtain credit.

The Importance of Establishing a Good Credit History

Even with poor credit, you will be able to finance many purchases such as a home or vehicle. However, good credit has certain advantages. Those with a high credit score receive prime rates on home loans and car loans.

For some, low rates may not be a huge deal. Yet, low interest rates on loans can potentially save you hundreds each month. Moreover, having good credit unlocks the door to better financing alternatives.

Similarities Between having no Credit and Bad Credit

Unfair as it may be, some lenders group those with no credit and individuals with poor credit into the same category. This makes it harder for young people and those trying to establish credit. Individuals with poor credit made certain mistakes that justify a lender's reluctance. On the other hand, those with no credit history have zero credit mistakes. So, why do some lenders deny credit to those with no credit history?

In a nutshell, before granting a credit card or loan, lenders will review credit reports to examine past relationships with other creditors. It is a way to determine an applicant's likelihood of repaying funds. If you have no credit history, lenders become uncertain. Instead of taking a gamble, they rather deny an application.

Getting Approved for a Bad Credit Credit Card

Getting approved for a bad credit; credit card is easy. The tricky part is finding a lender that specializes in this sort of credit. Use the internet to your advantage. Many bad credit; credit card lenders offer online applications and instant approvals. If you are hoping to build a good credit history, this is one of the easiest approaches.

There are two types of bad credit; credit cards. If you are approved for an unsecured card, you may receive an initial low credit limit. However, as you maintain regular payments, the creditor may gradually increase the spending limit. With a secured credit card, applicants must open a saving account with the lender. In the event that you decide to stop making payments, this account serves as collateral.

Chapter 11: Credit Scores: What is it About and What Makes a Good Credit Score?

Imagine yourself applying for a car loan, you have the money and you have the right job to pay the loan back before the due date. However, even if you have the right job and the money for it, you still haven't been approved for the loan. This will make you wonder why.

In the United States and UK, having money and having a high salary isn't everything. You have to consider one important thing that will have significant impact in your daily life. This important thing is used by creditors, such as banks and credit card companies to determine if you will likely pay back what you borrowed from them. This important thing is called the credit score or your credit rating.

If you were delinquent in paying your bills or loans in the past, you should expect to have a low credit score. Everything about your credit history will determine if you will get a high credit score or not. This is why it is important for you to settle those bills or loans on time in order to avoid getting a negative credit report from the creditors you borrowed money from.

For example, if it took you a long time to pay for your credit card bills, the credit card company will issue a report to credit reporting agencies that will state that you haven't been paying your bills on time, or you still have a debt to pay to their company. This will result in lowering your credit score.

You have to realize the fact that credit scores are very important in today's society. Even phone companies are now taking a look of their future subscriber's credit score to determine if they will likely pay the monthly phone bills or not. With a bad credit score, just simply getting a phone line hooked up in your house can be a difficult thing to do.

Lenders, such as banks and credit card companies also takes a look at your credit score to determine if you will be approved for the loan or the credit card or not. Having a high credit score will open a lot of credit opportunities for you. People with high credit score have a much easier time when applying for a low interest credit card and also for a low interest loans. This is because creditors are sure that they will likely pay their debts on time.

In order to get higher numbers, you should pay all your debts in time. What this means is that whatever loans or bills you have lying around in your home, you have to pay it in order to gain points in your credit score. If you don't, then your credit score will continue to decline and will also leave you in a far greater amount of debt.

Always remember that having a good credit score is a must. If you have a 725 credit score, you are well on your way to become a credit worthy person. Increase your score and gain access to the best loan and credit card deals possible.

Chapter 12: Credit Score Scale Revealed Just for You

What is the credit score scale and how do you know whether you have a good or bad credit rating? Well, the credit score scale may seem dark and mysterious, but it really isn't all that complicated. Here is what you need to know about your credit score and the credit score scale.

The credit score scale ranges from three hundred (300) to eight hundred and fifty (850). That means that if you are alive and there are records of you, there is no way you can have a credit score less than 300. If you have only a little bit of debt, you have had it for a long time (many years), and you have never missed a payment or been late with a payment, and you have an income, you might just have the perfect score of 850. Of course, very few people have either the lowest or the highest possible score; just about everyone falls somewhere between the two extremes.

If you want to fall at the very top level of the credit score scale, you should shoot for a rating of at least 720. At one time in the not too distant past, you may have been considered at the top of the game is your score was above 680, but no more. Just about every lender gives the best terms and interest rates only to those whose credit score falls above 720 on the scale.

If you know you have only some minor issues in your background that will negatively impact your credit history, you may fall somewhere between 680 and 720. If that is where you land on the credit score scale, you can probably find a bank or other lender who is willing to give you a decent loan that won't cost you an arm and a leg in interest.

If your score is between 630 and 679, you may find that you have to settle for loans that are not as flattering as those offered to the folks at the top of the credit score scale. In fact, some lenders may not be willing to offer you a loan at all. Most likely, though, you will be able to secure a loan if you really need one, are diligent about finding a lender, and are willing to pay a higher interest rate.

If your ranking is below 630 on the credit score scale, you will probably have a very difficult time getting a home mortgage or loan for a new car. Before you consider applying for these types of loans, you should definitely get a copy of your credit report and make sure that any mistakes are cleared up, and you should definitely make as many improvements to your credit score scale rating as possible.

In addition, remember that these are only guidelines, and that the policies of different lenders vary. What one bank considers "too risky" may be within the acceptable limits of another lender. So it also pays to shop around for the best deal you can get, no matter where you fall on the credit score scale of life.

Chapter 13: Credit Free Score

In the United States, your credit score is everything. It is something that you should take care of or if you don't, getting a phone, cable or gas line hooked up in your home can be difficult to do. There are also certain companies that take a look at your credit score first before they even hire you. Even if you are qualified to do the job, a low credit score can ruin it all for you.

Your credit score is also analyzed by creditors, such as banks and credit card companies. Just try to imagine that you need to get a loan to start your own business, with a low or bad credit score, you have a lesser chance of getting that loan approved or you may get it approved but with high interest rates. The same thing goes when you apply for a credit card. Credit card companies or banks that issue credit cards will first take a look at your credit score before they can get your application approved. A high credit score means that you have a greater chance of getting the best credit card deals with a lot of features and also with low interest rates for your every purchase using a certain credit card.

Even if you are applying for a mortgage, a car loan and other kinds of loans, your credit score will play a very important role in it. This is why it is very important for you to have a high credit score and maintain it that way or increase it.

Credit scores are calculated in the following factors:

Punctuality of payments – This will be 35% of the calculation. If you pay your bills on time or before the due date, your credit score will tend to be higher.

Capacity used – This will amount to 30% of the calculation of your credit score. It will contain a ration between the current revolving debts to total available revolving credit. If you use your credit card and if you don't use its entire credit limit, you will get a higher credit score.

1. Length of credit history – This will amount to 15% of the calculation of your credit score.

2. Types of credit used – This can affect 10% of your total credit score.

3. Recent search for credit or the amount of credit obtained recently – This will amount to 10% of the total calculation of your credit score.

Surprisingly, not many people know their credit score and often end up wondering why they got denied for their loan or credit card application. You can easily obtain a copy of your credit report by requesting for it from the credit reporting agencies. They will be able to provide you with a free calculation of your credit score every year. It is also a great way to find out if there are any errors in your credit report that may be causing you to have a low credit score. You can request it to be fixed in order to let you have a higher credit score than before.

Always remember that your credit score is an important factor of your life. Keep it high and you will get better deals on loans, and credit cards.

Chapter 14: How to Improve your Credit Score the Easy Way

Many people tend to neglect the fact that credit scores are very important in today's society. This simple three-digit number will significantly affect how you live your life and also your financial status.

By having a good credit score, you will be able to have access to the best loan and credit card deals available today. It will also be an important factor when you want to get a phone line hooked up in your home. Also, some companies prefer to hire people with good credit scores.

Now that you know how important a credit score is, you need to know what credit score is all about and how you can have a good credit score or at least improve your credit score.

Firstly, a credit score is a three-digit number that creditors look at to determine if you are credit worthy. What this means is that this is what most creditors base upon if you will be approved for your loan or credit card application. This will tell them that you will likely pay the loan or the credit card bills on or before the due date.

If you don't pay your bills on time, you will have a bad credit score or credit rating. This is because creditors will report to credit reporting agencies about your activities regarding how you pay your bills. This will serve as a record of your paying habits. The credit report will then be available to other creditors you try to borrow money from or try to apply for a credit card from.

If you have a bad credit history, the chances of you getting that application approved will be slim. Or, you can get a loan or credit card application approved but it will usually contain a high interest rate because you are deemed too risky to lend money to.

This is the reason why you need to improve your credit score in order to have access to the best loan and credit card deals available. Not only that, it will be easier for you to get a job, rent an apartment or even get a phone line hooked up because companies that offer these things will be sure that you are credible or is credit worthy.

The first thing you have to do when you try to improve your credit score is by cutting of the sources of negative credit reports about you. To do this, you need to pay your previous delinquencies or pay off your overdue loans. This will not significantly improve your credit score but it is a good step in cutting off the negative reports that will make your credit score much worse than it already is.

Now that you eliminated the negative sources of the reports, the next step is to improve your credit score. There are several ways to do this. The first one is request for a copy of your credit report from the three major credit reporting agencies. By doing this, you will be able to know about your credit status and also know whether there are any errors in it. For example, if the credit report contains an unpaid debt that you have previously paid before, send a letter containing a request to fix it and also send a copy of the proof that you already paid the debt in full. Errors like this can and will significantly lower your credit rating or credit score.

The best thing you can do to improve your credit score is to pay your bills on time. By doing this, you will make a positive credit report and therefore, will result in higher credit score.

Always remember that it is you who will determine whether you get a good credit score or not. By paying your obligations on time, you will be able to improve your credit score.

Chapter 15: Credit Score Chart
How to Interpret Your Numbers

A credit score chart answers the question "what is a good credit score?" Unfortunately, there is not a uniform answer to this question. Scores range between 300 and 850 with higher being better. While imperfect, a credit score chart will tell you whether your score is a good one or not.

The credit score chart given by various analysts agree that the cut off for excellent is either 770 or 760. Freddie Mac, Smart Money, and PBS's Frontline all agree that 770 is the cut off for "A+ Credit." Fair Isaac (the company that compiles credit reports) and MSN Money peg the number at 760.

People who score in the mid-700s on the credit score charts should also qualify for good interest rates and many types of credit offers. Lending Tree and Bank rate agree that scores between 650 and 760 qualify you as having above average credit. Fannie Mae says that a score of 740 makes you an excellent risk for a home mortgage.

The average credit score for prime deals in the United States is 733. TransUnion, a major reporter of credit scores reports that a score of 730 is "very good." This also applies in the UK.

The average credit score overall in the United States is 723. CBS reports that anything above 720 means that you don't really have to work on your score because you will be lumped in with higher scoring individuals by lenders.

As you fall lower on the credit score chart, though, you will start to have trouble in the form of higher interest rates. For instance, the Fannie Mae Foundation reports that a score of 675 can put you in a higher risk category for getting loans. 43 percent of minority home loan applicants have scores below 679 compared with just 32 percent of white applicants.

Newsweek advises people that if your score falls below 680, you should work with a credit rescorer when trying to get a home mortgage loan. The U.S. government's Office of Thrift Supervision points out that score below 680 usually do not qualify for prime lending rates on the credit score chart. 660 tend to be the bottom mark for banks being sure you will repay the loan.

When you fall below 600 on the credit score chart, you are considered a high risk according to the Dallas Morning News. Both Fair Isaac and the Consumer Federation of America agree that scores below 600 could make it difficult to get loans. CNN/Money says that a score below 600 could trigger a universal default clause in your loan.

Fair Isaac calls anything below 550 "awful."

While looking at this credit score chart, you can see that there are slight variables in what constitutes a "good," "average" or "bad" credit score. A 10 point variable can make a difference in interest rates at

different banks, which is why it is a good idea to shop around. Your credit score chart is merely a guide to credit, not an indication of absolute cut-offs.

Chapter 16: Credit Score Ranges the Good and the Bad in Your Numbers

Many people wonder what the credit score ranges are. They have heard that "good" credit can mean lower interest rates while "bad" credit can lock you out of various types of loans. But even if they know their actual score, they don't know where they fall on the credit score ranges.

The reason for this confusion is, in part, that there is no clear definition for what the credit score ranges are.

Credit scores fall on a spectrum between 300 and 850. Each lender determines individually how they will price loans with everyone wanting to secure higher scoring individuals. But, this range can vary.

For instance, Freddie Mac, Smart Money, and PBS's Frontline all agree that 770 is the cut off for "A+ Credit" while CBS reports that anything above 720 means that you don't really have to work on your score because you will be lumped in with higher scoring individuals by lenders.

Bearing that in mind, here is some general guidelines for credit score ranges.
1. Scores above 760 qualify you for the best rates at most lenders. You will also qualify for the premium credit card deals.
2. Scores between 720 and 760 will get you good

rates at lenders. The difference between a 800 score and a 730 score will be about $30 a month on a $200,000 loan.
3. 3.Scores between 680 and 720 will still qualify you for prime rates. You should also have no trouble getting credit cards in this credit score ranges.
4. Between 600 and 680, you will start to see an increase in interest rates. You should still qualify for credit card offers in general, but they won't be the premium ones.
5. Below 600 and you start having significantly higher interest rates.
6. 6.If you fall below 500, you may not qualify for unsecured loans at all.

Here is a breakdown of what sample interest rates could be on a 30 year fixed rate mortgage as of right now and what a monthly payment on a $200,000 mortgage would be for those credit score ranges according to Bank rate:
1. 780 – 5.8% - $1173
2. 730 – 6.0% - $1199
3. 680 – 6.4% - $1250
4. 630 – 6.8% - $1304
5. 590 – 9.8% - $1785 – Big Jump!
6. Bank rate doesn't calculate below 500

There is a difference between a top credit score and one at the bottom. This can result in a $545 a month extra payment. Over the life of a 30 year loan, that is close to $200,000 in extra interest paid.

There are things you can do to raise your credit score.

If you are thinking about buying a home in one year, make all of your bill payments on time. Your bill repayment history composes 30 percent of your credit score. Pay down all of your credit cards and other revolving credit. Make sure that toward the end of the year, you have no more than 50 percent of the total credit on any of the cards utilized. If you are going to close some credit card accounts, cancel the newer ones first. The length of your credit history on any one account matters.

Understanding credit score ranges can be important if you want to take out any kind of loan.

Chapter 17: Credit Score Range Why the Numbers Matter More Than You Think

The credit score range is a number between 300 and 850 that determines everything from whether you qualify for a mortgage to whether you get a job. Here are seven areas where your credit score range comes into play:

1.   Qualifying for a mortgage – If you have a credit score range above 620, you qualify for a regular mortgage.   Below 620 and you are pushed into a subprime mortgage.   If your score is above 720, you should be able to qualify for the best rates available.

2.   Leasing an apartment – Landlords run your credit when they are deciding whether to lease you an apartment or house.   That is because it is very expensive to evict a tenant.   They look at other factors besides your score such as past rental history, but you should know where you fall on the credit score range before filling out a lease application.

3.   Getting your utilities turned on – The electric company is interested in whether you pay your credit card bills because that is a good indicator of whether you will pay them.   If you have a score in the low credit score range, be prepared to pay a hefty deposit to get your utilities turned on at a new place.

4.   Obtaining a cell phone – It seems like everyone has a Bluetooth attached to their ears today.

But if your score falls into the low credit score range, you can say goodbye to any kind of phone unless you have a co-signer. People can rack up huge bills calling and texting their friends, so the cell phone companies want to make sure that you can pay your bills.

5.   Getting life or home insurance – This one is odd. There seems to be an inverse relationship between bad credit and good risk for insurance companies. Nobody is sure why it exists, but insurance companies are starting to pull credit reports to determine if you qualify for their products and at what rates. People who have bad credit sometimes pay 150% more than people with good credit on their car insurance.

6.   Starting a business – Many people who start a business need small business loans or personal lines of credit. In this depressed economy, more people want to start their own business rather than risk taking a job with a company. But, if you have a number in the low credit score range, you could have problems getting the loan to start your business.

7.   Okay, so you have decided that the financing is not there to start a business, so you hit the classifieds looking for a job. But, after you go on several interviews that you thought went well, you still haven't landed a position. It may be that the economy is tough right now. But it could also be that your low credit score is dragging you down. Employers are increasingly looking at credit scores to determine whether individuals would make responsible employees.

So, there you have seven examples of how high and low credit score ranges can affect your life.

Chapter 18: Credit History Repair Tips

There are plenty of very simple credit history repair tactics you can use to give your credit score a quick boost. If you are thinking about applying for new credit, then spending a little time getting your finances in order could help your chances of getting your application approved.

While there has been a lot of credit history repair tips focused on finding and correcting any errors on your credit report, it should be noted that a large percentage of people with bad credit don't have any erroneous listings. If you happen to find an entry on your report that shouldn't belong to you or has been listed in error, then you may dispute the entry and have it removed.

A more likely cause for a bad credit score is a history of late payments or missed payments on bills and loans. As your conduct with your financial responsibilities accounts for 35% of your total credit score, this is usually the section that can reduce your score most quickly.

The good news is; it's also the sector of your score that you can use some credit history repair tactics to improve rapidly.

Missed Payments and Late Payments

If you have any delinquent accounts showing more

than one missed payment, you should find a way to catch up those payments immediately. Do whatever it takes to catch up those missed payments and you will be rewarded with an instant boost to your credit score as each of your creditors reports this positive activity.

You may also find that your repayment amounts will be reduced as your creditors will no longer be able to charge you penalty fees and overdue interest rates. This can help your budget at the same time as offering some credit history repair assistance.

Reduce Outstanding Balances

How many of your existing credit cards are maxxed out with balances at the same level as the available limit? Your balances as they relate to your limits form 30% of your total credit score calculations. Reducing them even a little can give you a quick credit score boost.

Hold a yard sale. Find some unused items in your home to list for sale on eBay. Take on a part time weekend job to raise your income temporarily.

Beating Your Creditor's Reporting System

Here is a quick credit history repair tip. Your creditors report your repayment activity once a month. They base their information on whether you made your minimum payment amount by the due date or not.

Based on this monthly reporting system, it is possible to beat your creditor's reporting system and force them to report more positive activity than you have actually made and it is easier than you think.

Take your monthly payment amount and divide it by four. Let's assume you need to pay $190 per month. Divide that figure by four and your new weekly payment will be $47.50. Pay this amount on the same day every week.

By the end of the month, your creditors will be forced to report extra payment activity, which gives you a quick, easy boost to your score. The smaller amounts are easier to budget for each week too.

If you are serious about working on some quick credit history repair tactics, then work on these simple things you can do yourself for free. You will be helping to fix your bad credit and you will also be learning some financially responsible behaviour that will help stop you getting into the same situation again in future.

Chapter 19: What is Bad Credit Debt Consolidation?

Bad credit and debt consolidation go hand in hand; if you owe money, you are summoned to courts if you can't follow through with payments. If you have borrowed for a mortgage, a car, or a personal loan; which are secured loans in most instances and the loans' obligations are not met, you may be subpoenaed to court. Any courtroom is demanding, and many of the courts will consider both sides offensive. On the other hand, the participant concerned in negligence is frequently judged as untrustworthy. If you want to keep away from stressful situations, then it is imperative to construct shrewd decisions ahead of spending cash you don't have.

Avoiding court judgments, lawsuits, liens and other penalties is central to meeting repayments on your monthly debt. If you stumble on a corner in your life where you get a glimpse of difficulties required to meet these demands, you may want to glimpse into debt consolidation solutions obtainable that can remove you from harm's way.

If you are repaying credit on your home, you may want to consider selling your home. You could also search for a lower rate of interest loan and lower monthly instalment loan combined. Few mortgage loans will include a debt consolidation solution into the agreement.

When you already feel indebted and your bills are then sent to collection agencies you will become even more stressed. Once you are in the hands of collection agencies, be aware that most of these people could care less how they get their money. Some have even sent personnel to debtor's doors claiming to be the law. This is illegal, but debtors often fail to stay current with the laws; rather they are only worrying about how to pay their debts.

Be advised that it is illegal for creditors to call you before and after certain hours of the day. Finally, it is also illegal for creditors to call you, threatening to take you to court.

If you have bad credit and need to consolidate your debt, you should know your rights, so you can avoid being bullied by your creditors.

Chapter 20: The Basics of Debt Consolidation and Refinance

Mortgages are secured loans that are given to first time buyers, homeowners and people who have bad credit. The loans refinanced for debt consolidation are loans offered against the equity of your home. Once you are accepted for the loan, you must repay the debt, which will include interest rates. Some refinancing loans have additional fees attached. The secured loans have collateral attached, means that if you fail to make payments, you are subject to foreclosure or repossession. The bank will come and take your home and sell it for the amount you owe.

This is why it is wise to make sure you know what you are getting into if you plan to refinance to consolidate your debts. Some loans permit buyers to repay the loans in 25 years, while others allow 30 repayments. Few of the lenders available on the Internet that offer refinance loans for consolidation of debts are aware that people go through hard times- or at least they don't deal with people directly enough to actually feel this hardship through talking to them.

On the loans that offer lower interest rates, combine payments for debt consolidation. If you can manage to pay for the loan in the time stipulated, it is likely that you will take less time to pay back the loan amount borrowed. Once you find a lender to refinance your mortgage and combine your bills for debt consolidation, you will receive a loan based on capital and interest.

The Repayment loans for refinancing and consolidation make it easy, since the lenders will combine the interest and repayments into one monthly instalment. Still, few lenders will allow you to repay the interest rates only; however, be aware that these types of loans do not combine your payments for consolidation; rather they put you at risk in some instances.

Still, there are several types of loans available that will help you refinance for debt consolidation, so keep an open mind and mull over your choices carefully before you make a final decision.

Chapter 21: Getting a Loan for Your Loan

Credit card debt consolidation is regarded as the first step towards getting rid of credit card debt. Credit card debt consolidation loan is one of the ways of consolidating credit card debt. Besides, credit card debt consolidation loan, you can also go for balance transfer to another credit card.

In fact, due to the publicity by credit card suppliers, balance transfers seem to be more talked about than credit card debt consolidation loan. Some people kind of forget about credit card debt consolidation loan being available as a method of credit card debt consolidation. However, credit card debt consolidation loan too is important to consider when going for credit card debt consolidation.

So what do we mean by credit card debt consolidation loan?

Put simply, credit card debt consolidation loan is a low interest loan that you apply for with a bank or financial institution in order to clear off your high interest credit card debt. So credit card debt consolidation loan too is based on same principle as balance transfers i.e. moving from one or more high interest debts to a low interest one.

The credit card debt consolidation loan has to be paid back in monthly instalments and as per the terms and conditions agreed between you and the dispenser of credit card debt consolidation loan.

Credit card debt consolidation loan, in general terms, is an unsecured loan i.e. doesn't require you to pledge any security.

However, if you have a really bad credit history and you want go for credit card debt settlement using credit card debt consolidation loan, the credit card debt consolidation loan will take the form of a secured credit card debt consolidation loan.

This type of credit card debt consolidation loan requires you to pledge a security e.g. the home owned by you or something else that has a value which is comparable to your credit card debt consolidation loan amount. So, worse the credit rating, the more difficult it is to get a credit card debt consolidation loan.

Though balance transfers and credit card debt consolidation loans have the same objective behind them, the credit card debt consolidation loans are sometimes considered better because you end up closing most of your credit card accounts which have been the main culprit in landing you in this difficult situation.

However, balance transfers have their own advantages which are not available with credit card debt consolidation loans. Choosing between credit card debt consolidation loan and balance transfer is really a matter of personal choice.

Chapter 22: Is there Any Such Thing as Free Debt Consolidation

Free debt consolidation! The fact is, nothing in life is free, which is exactly why you should be dubious of any advertisements that claim to offer "free" debt consolidation. In most instances, you can get a free quote or else a first-time counselling session. And in most instances, the first-time counselling session is to lure you into the company's agreement.

Debt consolidation is a procedure that can take years to hash out. In most case, people with bad credit or current debt problems often believe there is no way out. They may go online and find a source that will help reduce their debts, believing that the amount of their debts is lower. Since few companies will lead many to believe this is true, it is important that you know that the debt consolidation companies are only reducing your rates of interest.

If you own a home and want to use the equity to refinance, you may want to understand that a good number of the Home Equity Loans will actually land you deeper in debt. Once you are bound to the contract, you will find the complications are more frustrating than when you first applied for the loan.

I brought this up because many homeowners will refinance their homes without looking into the details first, believing they are consolidating their bills. They may feel they are getting something free, since the amount on the mortgage appears reduced. However, if you take out a loan to consolidate your mortgage, you are only stepping into another debt.

Be advised that some mortgage contracts stipulate that if you refinance your home during the contract agreement, you may face penalties, which may include paying off your first home, your second home, and the interest rates included. Therefore, if you are considering debt consolidation, consider the entire picture first-and don't ever fall for the bogus claim that any debt consolidation will actually be free.

Chapter 23: Bad Credit Loan - How to Get the Best Interest Rate

Bad credit loans are in high demand. And if you do any research on "bad credit loan", you will find plenty of advice on how to get the lowest interest rate. You will also find plenty of people willing to give you a bad credit loan, but you did be making a mistake to accept it.

Unfortunately, most of what you will find approaches the problem from the wrong direction. The way to get the VERY best interest rate on a bad credit loan is usually overlooked or concealed altogether.

But before we continue, let's digress briefly and look at how significantly the higher rate for a bad credit loan affects the borrower.

Let's say you want to buy a house, but have bad credit. No matter how diligently you shop for a lender, you are still charged a higher interest rate for a bad credit loan than if you had good credit.

With good credit, you might get a mortgage loan at 6% interest. But a bad credit loan will cost you closer to 12%. Assuming you get a $100,000 mortgage over 30 years, the difference you did pay in interest amounts to a monstrous $154,461.60 MORE because you have bad credit. That is over 1½ times the loan itself!

Now getting back to our original problem, how can you get a better interest rate for a bad credit loan? The answer is probably not what you were expecting.

The solution is to "think outside the box." The way to get a bad credit loan with the best interest rate is to NOT get one! Instead, spend a couple of months fixing your bad credit, and then look for a "good credit loan" instead.

This answer probably comes as something of a shock to you. More than likely, several objections to this approach will come to mind.

1. "I need a loan NOW" or "It is not worth my while to wait until I repair my credit."

Oh really? Well, is it worth a savings of $150,000 or more? Granted you may not be looking for a $100,000 loan. But even if you want to borrow only $10,000 or so, the better rates you will enjoy with good credit will still save you several thousand dollars.

2. "Fixing my credit will take too long, or it just isn't possible."

It is often possible to make very a significant improvement in your credit rating in just a few months, and in some cases as little as 30 days.

3. "I don't know how to repair my credit and can't afford to hire a credit repair agency"

For a fraction of the cost of a professional agency,

you can purchase a good book on credit repair that will walk you through the whole process.

4. "Do-it-yourself credit repair is too difficult" or "I don't think I can repair my own credit"

Don't be intimidated by the idea of fixing your own credit. If you can write a few letters, address, stamp, and mail them you can repair your own credit.

Your decision comes down to this; you have two choices.

1. You can spend some time (maybe a LOT of time) shopping for a bad credit loan with the lowest possible rate, and still end up paying thousands (even tens of thousands) more in interest.

2. You can spend some time fixing your credit and spend those thousands on your family's needs, instead of paying them to your lender.

Do you really think your lender needs your hard earned money more than you and your family need it? Anybody can work on fixing their own credit. That's right, anybody!

Get a good book on credit repair and get started TODAY!

Chapter 24: Bad Credit! No Problem With Bad Debt Homeowner Loans

People with bad debt include people who have the history of bad credit. What bad credit means is that the borrower fails to meet the terms of the loans, which were initially agreed upon by the borrower and the creditor. This subsequently results in getting the borrower a bad credit score, and hence the bad credit. A credit score is a 3 digit figure usually ranging between 300 and 720 which depicts a borrower's credit worthiness at a point of time.

Usually, people with bad credit face a lot of problems in getting any type of loan. But, with bad debt homeowner loans, that problem has been put to rest. The bad debt homeowner loans are specifically designed to help people who have the problem of bad credit.

Anyone who wants to take the bad debt homeowner loans has to fulfil two conditions to make himself eligible for the loan.

1. The potential borrower should have a bad credit history i.e. he should be a bad debtor.
2. The second condition is that the borrower must be a homeowner i.e. he must have a home of his own in order to apply for the loan.

Both the conditions are required to be fulfilled in order to avail the bad debt homeowner loans.

Bad debt homeowner loans are no different in quality from any of its counterparts. They are just as beneficial and provide the equal amount of effectiveness to the borrowers. With bad debt homeowner loans the borrowers will find same loan options i.e. choose between a secured loan or an unsecured loan and other options that any other loan provides. Although, one slight disadvantage that can be attributed to the bad debt homeowner loans is that they may carry a rate of interest which may be higher than usual. But, then they compensate that with the fact that they provide the borrower with an opportunity to redeem their reputation, if he can meet the required terms of the loans that are agreed upon. This allows the borrowers to get the normal terms for their loans.

To apply for the bad debt homeowner loans, the borrower must possess a document showing his credit ratings and credit score. If they are not present then it can be taken through various credit rating agencies in the UK or US. Few of those being:
1. Experian
2. Equifax
3. Trans union

These or any other credit rating agency recognized by the lenders in UK or US can be requested to make your credit report.

People who want to apply for bad debt homeowner loans can apply for them by following the same procedure that any other loan warrants. And once they get a worthwhile deal they can apply for the loan. People applying for this loan must be careful about the finer details of the loan.

Chapter 25: Bad Credit Home Financing: Is It Possible to Buy a Home With Bad Credit

At one point in time, having bad credit made it extremely difficult to get a home loan. Fortunately, things have changed, and many people with less than perfect credit are obtaining home loans with decent rates. Getting a home loan with bad credit is doable. However, you must be willing to seek out lenders that offer bad credit loans.

Reasons to Consider Purchasing a New Home

Homeownership is beneficial for several reasons. Individuals who rent their homes or apartments are literally throwing away money. If your rent is $500 a month, in a year's time you would have spent $6000. Instead of making your landlord rich, this money could go towards paying a mortgage and building equity

Furthermore, if you own a home, you are eligible for certain tax deductions. Owning a home also makes it possible to get extra cash by tapping into your home's equity. Home equity loans and lines of credit are perfect for home improvements, unexpected expenses, debt consolidation, etc.

Choosing a Lender for a Bad Credit Mortgage

Be aware that not all lenders will offer loans to people with bad credit. Although many mortgage companies have started offering sub-prime mortgage loans, some lenders will not approve an application if your credit score falls short of their minimum requirements.

Because credit blemishes are common, and the average household carries a large credit card balance, many lenders have begun offering loan programs for all credit types. These loans also benefit those unable to save for a down payment or closing fees.

Tips for Getting Approved for a Bad Credit Mortgage

If you are hoping to get approved for a home loan with bad credit, you may qualify for a better rate if you fix credit problems beforehand. Improving your score by as little as ten points may make you eligible for a slightly lower rate.

Additionally, get multiple quotes by using a mortgage broker. Brokers can help you locate many sub-prime lenders that offer bad credit mortgages. When completing a quote request, choose a broker that does not review credit. If your credit is evaluated by four different lenders, it may decrease your score.

Instead, provide an accurate credit description. It may help to check your personal credit report before applying. Once you obtain at least four offers from different mortgage lenders, compare the quotes, and pick a lender. Complete the loan process by submitting an official loan application. The chosen lender will check your credit before finalizing the loan.

Chapter 26: Bad Credit Home Improvement Loans: Options for Getting a Loan With Poor Credit

Home improvements are costly. For this reason, many homeowners choose to finance the project. There are many ways to raise funds to complete home improvements. Although some people choose to use a credit card or store charge card, high finance fees make it practically impossible to repay the balance. Instead, consider applying for a home improvement loan.

Advantages of a Home Improvement Loan

Getting an unsecured home improvement loan is difficult with good or bad credit. However, having bad credit will make it exceptionally hard. Fortunately, bad credit home improvement loans are available. The secret is finding a lender that is willing to offer reasonable rates.

Once you secure financing for a home improvement project, the money can be used to repair a roof, build a spare bedroom, home upgrades, and improve the living space. Some individuals with bad credit avoid financing a home project. While saving money for a home project is ideal, and a great way to remain debt free, this approach will prolong a home improvement project.

Ways to Obtain a Home Improvement Loan with Poor Credit

Before determining that a home improvement loan is unfeasible, contact several lenders and discuss your lending needs. In most cases, a bank or credit union will be unable to help you. On the other hand, if a bank offers sub-prime loans you may be a good candidate.

If you have a low credit score, you will not qualify for an unsecured home improvement loan. However, a lender may approve you for a secured loan. If seeking a small loan, consider securing the loan with a piece of property. A vehicle title may be sufficient to obtain financing.

For major home improvement projects, take advantage of your home's equity. Various lenders approve home equity loans regardless of credit. Of course, if you have poor credit, your interest rate will be slightly higher. Still, these rates are good in comparison to credit card rates.

If acquiring a home equity loan to finance a home improvement project, do not accept a loan without fully accessing your finances. Is another monthly payment affordable? If your finances are tight, avoid accumulating additional debt. A home equity loan is secured by your home. If you become unable to maintain timely payments, you risk losing your home and equity.

apter 27: Are There Loans for People With Bad Credit

Life is tough! Everyone gets the chance to learn this harsh fact when they take it upon themselves to move away from home and finance their own lifestyle. Suddenly there is rent, a car payment, insurance bills, medical insurance, dental plans and more.

Suddenly you are using credit cards to keep up with the countless bills being tossed in your face. Naturally this bad process leads to massive credit card debt and all of the sudden you have a mortgage to worry about on top of that. Okay, the first thing you should not do is panic. Freaking out will get you nowhere. In reality, most of mankind is also grappling with the same monetary issues. Therefore there is no reason to feel alone. Fortunately even if your credit is poor, there are loans for people with bad credit available. The key is finding them and taking advantage of them.

While many individuals may have started with a common financial advisor in the past when they were in search of loans for people with bad credit, these days' things have changed. Sure, there are still financial advisors, but there is also the Internet at your disposal. Online you can learn a great deal about bad credit loans and effectively paying off hideous debt.

These online services for people with bad credit can

provide you with a plan that is beneficial to your particular situation. Consider the amount of debt you owe and when it all needs to be paid off by. Now take a peek at the percentage rates you are currently conforming to. Yep, you will probably be irked to say the least. Most likely there are helpful loans for people with bad credit to assist you now and help you bring those awful interest rates way down.

Do not make the mistake of waiting or not seeking out loans for people with bad credit immediately. The sooner the better. The key is to stop paying out major dough to high interest rates. This is how you are losing oodles of money! There is surely a bad credit loan out there to assist you. All you have to do is a bit of homework.

Chapter 28: Loans for People With Bad Credit

If you have had troubles paying your bills on time in the past you may think that no one will ever lend you money ever again. Nothing is further from the truth. There are plenty of loans for people with bad credit available and you can find one that suits your specific needs if you do a little homework.

Homeowners have some better options available than people who rent. This is because they can find loans for people with bad credit that are secured. A secured debt is beneficial to you because you will be offered more options than are available for an unsecured loan.

The secured loans for people with bad credit are more lenient about your past payment history than their unsecured counterparts. You will be more likely to get approved if the debt is secured. Meeting the eligibility criteria is much easier for these kinds of debts because you have more at stake.

The bank also benefits because it has some leverage when it comes to collecting on the debt. If you fail to pay back the debt then the bank has more recourse than it would with an unsecured loan. These loans for people with bad credit are wonderful for rebuilding your payment history and they are relatively easy to get.

You can also expect to be able to borrow more with the secured loans. The higher amount offered through these programs are very appealing to a lot of homeowners who want to re-establish credit. Monthly payments will be lower because the secured loans for people with bad credit can be repaid over a longer period of time.

There is a significant drawback to the secured loans for people with bad credit. Your home is at stake in the process. Failure to make good on the debt can cost you your home. The house is the security against the debt. This is a big step that has to be dealt with caution.

For those who are more attracted to the unsecured counterparts, you can still find a lender who will be more than happy to work with you. It is important to remember that these loans for people with bad credit will usually have a hefty annual percentage rate. This means that you will pay a lot more over the course of repayment than the amount of the loan itself.

Consolidation loans may be the best place for you to start. These loans for people with bad credit are the first steps to repairing damaged payment histories. Once you have re-established decent credit you can get just about any loan that you want at a reasonable percentage rate.

Chapter 29: Subprime Mortgages

It sounds terrible; subprime mortgage, but in reality it have many different benefits that other loans do not.

A subprime loan typically has a higher interest rate than other loans because the people who need it usually have a poor credit history or very low credit score.

These high interest loans do make people pay a lot more for a house they want but actually have some benefits.

There are many financial institutions that specifically deal with subprime lenders. This means they know how to help those with poor credit.

Some banks also offer prime and subprime mortgages because they know their community well and some areas just don't have the types of jobs that prime mortgages will need to ensure their monthly payments.

It can be embarrassing to go to a local bank if you live in a relatively small town so you may want to choose a subprime only lender.

A good benefit of a subprime mortgage is that you don't have to take the time to raise your credit score. This can take years of payments and credit building and many people just don't have the time for all of that.

They realize they made some late payments here and there but are past that and want to own a home. Not everyone with bad credit got it by not paying their bills on time.

Many times, wives and husbands who are irresponsible can annihilate their significant other's credit and even after divorce, it's still bad. A subprime mortgage to many people is a chance for a new beginning.

Chapter 30: Bad Credit Home Loan Financing - Take It to the Bank

It used to be pretty easy to get bad credit home loan financing. Countrywide specialized in these mortgages. But, we all know what happened to Countrywide – it went belly up and Bank of America was forced to buy up its bad assets. Therefore, bad credit home loan financing is less available today.

That does not mean you cannot get bad credit home loan financing. It just means you will have to dig a little deeper to find it.

The first thing you should do is determine whether you really are a subprime borrower. Many people are pleasantly surprised to find that they have better credit scores than they had thought. If your credit score is better than 620, you probably don't need bad credit home loan financing, you can get into a traditional mortgage.

Secondly, if you are on the border and you have credit between 580 and 620, try to raise your score. Get your credit report and challenge any inaccuracies. If you have any bad debts, make good on them in exchange for the lender marking them "paid in full" on your return.

But, if these tricks don't get you into normal mortgage territory and you still need bad credit home loan financing, go talk to a lender at your bank to get an idea of what you will pre-qualify for. If you have credit below the 580 mark, you may be unpleasantly surprised at how much the premium you will pay on the loan is.

If that is the case, then get on the internet and search for "bad credit home loan financing." There are many lenders who specialize in such loans. There are also services where you enter your basic financial information once and get several loan quotes. These are not firm offers because there are still variables such as your proving your financial information and the property you choose itself, but it should give you a good idea about whether you actually can qualify for a home.

You do have some things going for you right now, even if you have bad credit. There are millions of homes sitting vacant. Banks want to get these properties off of their books and are willing to go to extraordinary lengths, including bad credit home loan financing schemes, to sell these homes. Also, interest rates are currently low. So, even if you are paying a premium, it may be lower than it was a couple of years ago.

In addition, there is a nine month supply of new homes. Builders want to get rid of these properties. They may be able to offer you attractive rates so that entire tracts aren't sitting empty.

The good news is that if you get into a high interest rate bad credit home loan financing situation, you can get into a lower rate in as little as 24 months providing that you make all of your payments on time. In fact, one of the best ways to clean up your credit and raise your credit score is to buy a house and keep current on the payments.

If you are looking to buy a home, dig deep to come up with the best bad credit home loan financing.

Chapter 31: Mortgages for People with Bad Credit

The most important factor that determines whether a person is can get a loan for himself or not is the fact, whether his/her past credit history is stable enough or not. All factors depend on past record of handling credits.

A bad credit history implies that his/her appeal for a loan would be rejected and won't be met in most of the places. And the worst part is that, if the concerned individual in his/her past has ever been declared as bankrupt or had a foreclosure; then for sure the borrower would face difficulties when he tries to get a financing for a home mortgage purchase, home equity or second mortgage loan. But the gab that home loans are not available for people with bad credit history is just a baseless myth. Since these loans are available to people with bad credit history too. The way to find such a kind of loan is to be to be persistent in looking out for such kind of loans, because there are home mortgage loans for people with bad credit.

The basic problems involving, the process of procuring loan arises from the activities of sub-prime lenders. These are those lenders who actually work really hard for fetching loans for the people with bad credit background and low credit score and then they charge absolutely unreasonable price for the job.

Borrowers should be careful of borrowing money

from sub-prime lenders, as they can charge high interest rates which, comparatively are too high than the market rate. Not only this, but these lenders also charge unreasonable pre-payment penalties.

However, it's not absolutely impossible to find lenders who give out loans at reasonable rates and agreeable charges, to people who have a bad credit history. All a borrower needs to do is look around and talk to different mortgage brokers, which would prove to be helpful to find a lender that can get them an approved loan with a reasonable interest rate and fair terms of repayment.

Things that the borrower, should make sure about, are that he makes use of the lowest interest rate and terms possible. Specially a borrower with a bad credit history and bad credit score should make sure that he/she sends application for loans to a number of different lenders, since it would be sensible for him/her to make comparison between different mortgage loan quotes, so that he/she makes sure that they chooses the best one.

Chapter 32: A Refinance Mortgage Loan Can Make Sense for You

Are you looking for a way to finance your kids' educations? Do you dream of taking the vacation of a lifetime? Would you like to purchase a new vehicle and perhaps be able to deduct the interest from your federal taxes? Would you like cash for home improvements? Maybe you are interested in having a way to buy your new dream house while your current house is still on the market waiting to be sold? If any of these circumstances apply to you, you are probably thinking about getting a refinance mortgage loan.

What does it mean to refinance your mortgage?

As the name implies, it means that you renegotiate your loan. Usually, refinance mortgage loans are taken out by people who wish to tap into the equity they have built up by paying down the principal on their mortgage. For this reason, refinance mortgage loans are also sometimes referred to as home equity loans.

What exactly does it mean to have equity in your home? That means that your home is worth more than you owe. If the market value of your house is, for example, one hundred thousand dollars, but you only owe eighty-five thousand, you have fifteen thousand dollars worth of equity in your home.

Many lenders are willing to offer a refinance mortgage

loan if you have equity in your house, and you may choose to refinance to get cash for something you wants or need such as a vacation, home improvements, or a college fund. You may also decide to refinance simply because it makes good financial sense. A lot of times, people have to take less-than-ideal mortgage terms when they are buying their house, either because they have bad credit or little credit when they first take out their home loan.

As time goes on, however, you may have a better credit history or the prime interest rate may be lower than it was when you first bought. If the prime rate is lower, you are likely to be able to refinance your mortgage loan at a lower interest rate and show a significant savings with reduced monthly payments or a lifetime interest savings of thousands of dollars.

Does it make good sense to refinance your mortgage loan? For some people it does; for others, there is no real advantage. If you are considering tapping into your home's equity, be sure to discuss all your refinance options with a good financial adviser and understand what exactly the pros and cons are for your particular situation.

Many people find a refinance a viable alternative to taking out other costly loans that may not have the same tax benefits as a home equity loan. Some refinance mortgage loans even have a lower interest rate than government-backed student loans, so it pays to take a look at all your options and make the best decision for you.

Chapter 33: Home Equity Loan

In simple terminology, a home equity loan is a loan taken against your house. A home equity loan is also called a mortgage or a second mortgage. Another synonym for home equity loan is equity release schemes.

While taking a home equity loan you are actually borrowing the worth of your house. If the house is completely owned by you, then the term used for home equity loan is "mortgage", otherwise if your house is not fully paid off but has equity, it is called a "second mortgage". From now on I will use one term for both to facilitate better understanding. We will call them Home Equity Loans.

A home equity loan is an extra loan that you take against your home in addition to your mortgage; hence this is called a second mortgage. This enables a home owner to realize equity without refinancing the first mortgage. Most people are under the impression that the only way to raise cash is by selling their homes. However reality differs and factually one can take a second mortgage to free up the first mortgage also.

Equity is the difference between the amount you owe on your current home mortgage and the current value of your home. Furthering this definition, suppose you sell your home, the amount of cash left in your pocket after paying off the mortgage is called Equity. This equity when taken as a loan from a lender, without actually selling your home comes to be known as home equity loan.

Many lenders or loan companies allow you to borrow bigger amounts calculated by subtracting the balances of outstanding mortgages from 125% of the market value of your home. However the actual equity is the difference between appraised worth of your home and the balances of your outstanding mortgages.

There is no bar on how you can use the home equity loan. You can use it for any purposes as it suits you. A home equity loan is usually a one-time fixed interest rate loan, which is paid out at one go.

The rates of interest or the cost of the loan will depend on options you choose, the term of the loan and the amount; of course another important factor has always been your credit rating. The longer the term of the loan, the more you pay out as interest, also if the amount is more, the more interest you pay.

As always with any liabilities one undertakes certain words of caution are advised. Check all your options thoroughly before making a decision. Choose the amount carefully and take only what you need and specify the term which you think would be comfortable for you to repay in. No point accumulating liabilities in exchange for spending on pleasures or acquiring unnecessary assets.

Home equity loans are easily accessible to people with poor or bad credit rating since the lender is taking a lesser risk as the loan is secured against their home.

A Home Equity Loan usually means that you get the best interest rates on the loan, i.e. you get the loan at a lesser cost compared to other loans because of assured security, but one should always remember that the house is at risk lest you fail to repay the Home Equity Loan.

Chapter 34: Bad Credit Mortgage Loans Making the Dream of Homeownership Come True

Bad credit mortgage loans make the American dream of home ownership a possibility even for people with less than perfect credit scores. Subprime loans (also called second chance lending) are usually granted to people with credit scores of less than 680.

Subprime loans are generally required by people who have missed more than two payments in the last 12 months; have a judgment, foreclosure, or eviction against them; declared bankruptcy in the last 5 years; or have a generally defined high risk of default.

Back in the 1930s, the 30 year fixed rate mortgage was introduced as a financial instrument. Since then, the rate of home ownership has doubled and two-thirds of Americans own their own homes today. To expand the reality of homeownership to as many people as possible, sub-prime or bad credit mortgage loans came into being.

When you take out bad credit mortgage loans, be prepared to pay higher interest rates and fees. You may also have to take out extra insurance to ensure that the bank gets paid back. Be prepared for bad credit mortgage loans to be more difficult to get in 2011 than they were before the housing bubble burst. This is because there is less liquidity in the markets and the capital will flow first to those with better credit.

But that does not mean that bad credit mortgage loans do not exist. You just have to work a little bit harder to find them.

First off, you should clear up your own credit history to the extent possible. Get a copy of your credit report and dispute any inaccuracies. Pay off any bad debt and get the creditor to mark the bill satisfied in full on your credit report.

Then, start shopping for lenders. You are looking for a bad credit mortgage loans lender who will give you the best loan at the best rate with the fewest fees.

Be prepared to get into a loan for the short term as your chances of refinancing after 24 months are good. There are two reasons for this. The first reason is that after 24 months of regular payments, your credit will improve making regular loans more accessible.

But, the other reason is that by 2013, the credit markets are bound to have improved. You will have built equity in your home so the loan will be a secure investment for the bank. At that point, you can refinance into a more manageable loan.

Bad credit mortgage loans exist to allow people like you the benefits and security of owning your own home. These subprime loans are lifesavers for people who want to work their way back into normal credit. Generally within 2 to 3 years, a responsible borrower

will get into a regular loan rather than the bad credit
mortgage loans they started with.

Chapter 35: Where to Get a Bad Credit Loan Mortgage

If you have gone through a bankruptcy or have a less than stellar credit history, you may be concerned that you are never going to be able to buy the home of your dreams. It may take a little extra looking, and it may even cost a bit more, but there is such a thing as a bad credit loan mortgage that can help you realize your dream of homeownership even if your credit rating is not as high as you wish it were.

Not everyone is in total control of their credit histories all the time; there are numerous reasons for someone to have bad credit reports. Health issues and the medical bills that go with them, divorce, and job losses are all issues that people face in life, and sometimes those issues can adversely affect your credit history.

Your best bet when searching for a bad credit mortgage may be to consider leaving behind conventional financing and try instead to get a USDA, VA, or FHA loan in the U.S.

USDA loans may be the right solution for your bad credit loan mortgage if you have very little money to put down and if you want to purchase a home that is in a rural area. They may cover 100% of the cost of the home (sometimes even 102%), which is not as common as it has been in times past. It is also possible to get a fixed-rate loan through the USDA Rural Housing program, and it may not be necessary to carry private mortgage insurance (PMI).

VA loans are available to people currently serving in one of the branches of the armed forces and/or veterans. They are backed by the Veterans Administration, which makes lenders more eager to lend even if you have bad credit. The terms tend to be less costly than traditional mortgages, especially for those with bad credit. These loans are not available for investment property or mobile homes; they are only available for a property in which the borrower is going to live.

FHA loans are loans that are backed by mortgage protection insurance from the Federal Housing Authority. Even with bad credit, you may be eligible for an FHA mortgage loan. The FHA's goal is to allow as many people as possible to reap the emotional and financial rewards that come with home ownership, and they have been assisting with bad credit loan mortgages for many years. Even if you have good credit, and FHA loan is worth looking into, as the protection offered by the FHA allows lenders to loan money to borrowers who have very little money to use as a down payment on their little piece of heaven.

If you have had past credit difficulties, you should know that you are not alone; you should also know that there may be options available for you. Bad credit loan mortgages can be found and help you realize your dream of owning your own home.

Chapter 36: Real Estate Investing

There are many methods for building fortunes in the world today. One of the most accessible even for the common entrepreneur however is real estate investing. In fact, you will find many rags to riches stories are built by investing in the real estate marketing in one form or another if not many methods for investing in this lucrative but risky field.

Real estate is a great strategy for the investor who is willing to make the time to learn about the options, risks, and potential rewards for this type of investment process. Some of the more common real estate investments are the following:

1) Rental property. Property ordinarily gains value over time unlike many other investments that may rise and fall quickly and without warning. The problem is that far too few people can actually afford to hold and maintain multiple properties over an extended and indefinite period of time while waiting for the value to rise. Many property investors manage to overcome this by renting the properties to tenants during the time when the property values are rising. This allows the tenants to essentially cover the note on the property and makes the venture a little less risky though there are risks involved when dealing with tenants (such as property damage, failure to pay the rent, and possible legal woes-the good tenants generally outweigh the bad).

2) Pre-construction investment. This is a highly speculative and very risky sort of property investment that has booms and busts. Many investors recently discovered exactly how risky this endeavour actually is when the property 'bubble' went bust so to speak. The risks involved in this type of investment should not cover up the fact that many millionaires have been created through pre-construction investing and many more will be created in the future. Pre-construction investing, just as its name implies is a type of investment in which investors purchase 'options' on the property before ground is broken. This is very popular in high demand areas that are known to experience housing shortages as prices often rise quickly and the units are often sold before they are completed and any 'real' money exchanges hands.

3) Flipping houses. This is a type of property investment that has made leaps and bounds in the last few years thanks to the popularity of many popular home improvement and house flipping shows on cable networks in the last few years. More and more people have decided to pursue this sort of investment in hopes of creating big profits in a short amount of time and with minimal investment. The problem, of course, is that it always looks much easier on television than it is in person. Couple this with the fact that many people have unrealistic expectations when it comes to costs and ability and there are plenty of risks involved with this type of investment as well. For those who are successful however, there is the potential for great profit in a relatively short amount of time as these televisions shows indicate.

4) Buy and hold. As mentioned above, real estate tends to gain value over time. Even if the buildings are in desperate need of TLC and repair the very land they are standing on is more often than not gaining value as the years pass by. Purchasing large lots of land or even several houses and holding on to them for as long as possible before selling can often fund college educations for children, pay for weddings, or greatly supplement retirement funds. The longer these properties are held the better in most cases as this provides the greatest opportunity for the value of the property to increase.

5) Lease options. There are few people in this world who never experience rough spots financially. Many of these people are denied traditional home loans because of their inability to cover debts properly in the past. For this reason they are often willing to pay for the privilege of rebuilding their credit while working towards a path of home ownership. For these people, a lease option presents a workable and often valued solution. Those investors who are willing to take the risks often find the rewards are well worth those risks.

These are only some of the investment opportunities that exist for those who are interested in real estate for an investment avenue. There are commercial real estate endeavours that have the potential to bring in big profits as well as the development and planning of housing communities as well. Needless to say real estate investing offers many opportunities to the savvy investor.

Chapter 37: First Time Homebuyer a Great Time to Buy

Are you a first time homebuyer? If you are, you may be worried that this is not the right time to buy your first house; I mean, it is no secret that people are being foreclosed on and losing their homes left and right, and it is also no secret that we are in a rather bad economy right now. But now might just be the best time to buy a home for a lot of people, especially if you are a first time homebuyer.

First time homebuyers can have this as motivation: home prices are at an all-time low. That means that you can get a bargain price and much more house for the money than buyers were getting about seven or eight years ago when the real estate market was booming. It really is basic economics; there are more houses for sale than people who want or are able to buy them; therefore, supply is higher than demand and prices are low.

In addition to good prices, first time homebuyers can expect to have real estate professionals scrambling to get your business. Some are even offering incentives other than lower home prices. You may be able to negotiate a cruise, a car or truck, or some other compensation if you are willing to buy a house that has been on the market for a long time.

Some first time homebuyers fear that they may not be able to get a mortgage, but if you have a good credit rating, it really should not be a problem to get the loan you need. It is true that in light of the freewheeling loans being given in the past and the subsequent chaos in the housing industry, most lenders are being more particular about who can get a loan and who can't, but they are not locking the doors and refusing to make loans. Banks still want your business if you have a decent credit score and relatively secure job.

You may also be able to find a house that is owned by a bank or other lender, and they really do not want to own houses. They are in the business of lending money and conducting financial transactions. They are not in the home-selling business; therefore, they want to get rid of homes as quickly and easily as possible, which may reduce not only the price you pay but also the length of time it takes to push paperwork through.

If you are a first time homebuyer, it is natural to feel a little anxiety, but with careful planning and some god financial advice, you should feel confident that this is a perfectly acceptable time to be investing in the American dream of homeownership. Owning a home is still the best way to ensure stability for yourself and your children. Owning a home is still a decent investment, particularly now when prices are low. There is no doubt that home prices will rise again, and when they do, today's first time homebuyers can cash in by buying low and selling high.

If you have reasonably secure employment and a decent credit history, there is no reason you should not become a first time homebuyer when the time is right for you and your family.

Chapter 38: 101 Ways to Decrease Your Debt and Increase Your Credit

1. **Pay your bills first:** It's important to put the money aside to pay your bills as soon as you get paid. That way you will be sure to have enough money to pay them. Don't go out and buy things, not even groceries until you have put the money aside for your bills. Most of your day to day expenses are likely to have some flexibility in them, you can limit how much you spend on coffee a day or buy a less expensive cut of meat, but the power company wants all their money.

2. **Make your payments on time:** Every late payment can hurt you, and in more than one way. Many utility companies report your payments to the credit reporting agencies, so a history of late payments can hurt your credit score. It also costs you more if you pay late. Late fees may be small but when you are working on reducing debt, every dollar counts. Three dollars a month in late payment charges on three bills works out to over a hundred dollars a year.

3. **Write down what you spend:** Managing and paying down debt is all about taking control of your money. You cannot control what you do not know, so it is important to keep a journal of how much you are spending and what you are spending it on. Do it before you make your budget and you will be able to see what you really

121

do spend money on, rather than guessing and coming up short because you forgot to account for something when you wrote up the budget.

4. **Know your credit report:** Your credit report is your scorecard in the fight against bad credit. If you do not know where you stand it is hard to move forward. Most countries let consumers see their reports for free at least once a year. Take advantage of this, you might find a debt on there that you already paid which was not reported to the agency. Reports of unpaid debts can really hurt your credit, so it is important to make sure those are accurate.

5. **Pay creditors who report to agencies first:** Some creditors report each payment you make to credit reporting agencies, while others only report information if they send your debt to an outside collection agency. If you have to postpone one of your bills past the due date, it is always better for your credit score (all else being equal) if you pay the one that reports regularly as it will have the biggest impact on your credit score.

6. **Pay your bills when you have the money; don't wait until the due dates:** A lot of people think the due date on a bill is the day you are supposed to pay it, not the day by which the creditor wants to have received the money. Paying bills as soon as you get paid removes the temptation to take some of the money back to spend on something else. Once it is gone, so is

the temptation to take the money and spend it elsewhere.

7. **Ensure your creditors notify credit agencies when bills are paid:** If you do have unpaid bills, it is important not only to pay them but also to make sure those payments are reported to the credit agencies, otherwise those payments won't help repair your credit. Talk to the creditor about this, and if necessary do not hesitate to follow up with the credit reporting agency yourself.

8. **Always pay something:** Even if you cannot pay all of your bills at one time, always make a payment of some kind on each bill. This not only shows your good faith to the creditor by proving that you are not ignoring the debt, but it also reduces the amount you will have to pay when the next bill comes due. If one month is hard to pay now, two months will be harder to pay in future. Making partial payments helps reduce the effect of late payments piling up on each other.

9. **Make a budget:** Budgeting is an important part of controlling your money. It helps you see the big picture and gives you a plan with defined steps to focus on, reducing your debt and improving your credit into a plan of attack. Budgeting is the how of debt reduction; it is where you write down the plan you are going to follow to get your finances under control. You have to start somewhere, and budgeting is a good place to start.

10. **Save your pennies and other coins:** It is amazing how much money we carry around as loose change in our pockets, and it is money we often do not think of as money. Half the time it gets spent on a candy bar because we are bored rather than anything one needs. Turn it into an asset by dumping your change into a jar every night once you get home. It is amazing how fast it will add up, and that is money that can be used for emergencies, or to pay down a debt that suddenly jumped to the top of the pile.

11. **Communicate with lenders:** This is one many debtors ignore. Your creditors only want your money, and most of them are more than happy to work with you so long as they get their money in the end. The catch is that you have to keep them in the loop. Telling them what is going on and offering payment plans helps convince them that you are not planning to default on the debt. Yes they want their money, but that does not mean you have to put them in an adversarial role.

12. **Know your rights:** Both debtors and creditors have rights, but creditors are usually much more aware of their rights than debtors are. Knowing your rights gives you as a debtor a way to deflect harassing collection calls and a measure of control in the situation. It also lets you tell when an overzealous collection agent is making threats they cannot back up.

13. **Set goals:** Every task needs milestones, something to let you feel you are progressing and

prevent the enormity of the situation from becoming overwhelming. Repairing your credit and reducing debt is no different. Setting manageable goals like paying off one credit card within a year will help keep you focused and moving forward on debt reduction. If you are looking to build credit, getting a credit card within a year is a good goal. It does not matter what the goal is so much as making sure it is attainable and working towards it.

14. **Leave some money for extras:** No matter how much debt you are carrying, always make sure to put some money in the budget for extras and entertainment. Yes there are free alternatives to entertainment, but never having money for treats such as a five-shot Mocha, a night at the movies or a new book or CD is sure to frustrate you and get you off your budget. Put in some money, not a lot, but enough so that you can treat yourself on occasion and it will be a lot easier to stay on your budget.

15. **Pay cash:** Don't buy things with the swipe of a card if you can avoid it. Pay cash before using debit or credit. The thing about debit and credit payments is that the expenditure is invisible so you do not really notice how much you are spending. If you pay cash you have a much better feel for how much money you are spending which lets you keep more control of your money.

16. **It is not a good deal if it is more than you can afford:** How many times have you gone into a

store and seen a ten-pound bag of something at only twice the price of the two-pound bag? It may be a great deal, but it is not always a good buy. Remember, you are still spending more money, and that has to come from somewhere. Also, if you are not going to use it all before it goes bad you might find you have bought ten pounds and thrown away eight and then you are wasting money. Buy based on your needs, not just how good the deal looks.

17. **Pay off high rate cards first:** If you have got two credit cards that you need to pay off, take the one with the higher interest rate and pay it off first while making the minimum payment on the other card. Interest is lost money, so the faster you pay off the card with the higher interest the more debt you are losing for the same amount of money spent. Even a 2% difference in credit card interest rates can make a huge difference.

18. **Consolidate your loans:** Loan consolidation is a great tool if you have access to it. If you can get all your debts combined into one monthly payment you will often find you are paying everything off much sooner. Not only will a bank often give you a lower interest rate than credit cards, which means more of your money is going to reduce the debt rather than just service it, but making a single payment is usually cheaper than writing out half a dozen cheques every month.

19. **Cut up your credit cards:** An important part of getting out of debt is making sure you do not

incur more debt, and this is where cutting up your credit cards comes in. You can't cancel the account before you pay it off, but cutting up the card makes you that much less able to use it, especially if the CVN on the back isn't on your statement. Then you won't even be able to use it online. Part of taking control is reducing temptation.

20. **Ask to have your credit limit lowered:** Credit cards are useful to have, but it is important to stay out of trouble when using them. One way to keep control of your credit card spending is to keep a low limit like $500 on the card to make it that much harder to get into trouble. If you get a card with a high limit and are concerned you will run it up and not be able to pay, call the company and see if you can get the limit lowered to something you can keep ahead of.

21. **Watch out for introductory rates:** Lots of credit cards hit you with this one. They will advertise an absolutely fantastic interest rate for the first six months or year, then hit you with a massive rate increase that will send your payments skyrocketing. The introductory rate does not matter at all, what matters is the rate you will be paying over the long term.

22. **Store cards are easier to get:** It can often be easier to get a department store credit card than a major credit card, especially if you have little or no credit history. This can be a real help for people trying to build an initial credit history. Get

a store card and use it for a while before applying for a major credit card.

23. **Get a secured card:** If you have a really poor credit score and want to improve it, one option is to get a secured credit card. While it may look like a prepaid card, a secured card is different. With a secured card you send the provider money and they then open a line of credit equal to your deposit. Because they are extending you credit, even though it is secured by your deposit, it counts toward your credit score.

24. **Prepaid cards don't help your credit rating:** The only reason to get a prepaid card is to gain access to the credit card payment systems. Because they are debit and not credit cards they do nothing to repair your credit. However they do give you the ability to buy online at places that require a major credit card. However, if you have enough money to make the minimum deposit, get a secured card instead. It will affect your credit.

25. **Bankruptcy does not solve all debts:** There is a common misconception that bankruptcy is like a get out of debt free card. Unfortunately it does not always work that way. Bankrupts can still be liable for some debts, including taxes, child support and mechanics' liens. It provides relief from the worst pressures of debt, but does not eliminate it completely.

26. **Make deals when you can:** Collection agencies buy your debts at less than face value, and then

try to collect more. If you have money available, sometimes you can make a deal with the collection agency to accept less than the total outstanding as payment in full. It doesn't always work, but if you have some money, give it a try.

27. **Use a prepaid cell phone:** There are a few factors that make a prepaid cell phone a good idea when you are working on reducing your debt. The biggest one is not that it is cheaper than a regular post-paid plan, but rather that with prepaid you won't get the sudden large bills from going over your minutes that can wreck your budget and send bills spiralling out of control.

28. **Keep your word when making arrangements:** If you have to make arrangements to pay a bill rather than paying on time, you need to make sure they are ones you can keep. Often if you do renege on a partial payment arrangement the creditor might demand the full amount due immediately. Even if they don't you may be unable to make further deals with the same creditors if you need to.

29. **Credit counsellors can make things worse in the short run:** If you do go to a credit counsellor for assistance, they will often recommend that you cut off all contact with your creditors and go through them for all communications and payments. While this may sound like a good idea, it is important to be aware your credit rating may take a hit because of the missed payments this strategy will cause.

30. **Avoid the payday loan trap:** Payday loans are a quick fix and a bad idea. The U.S. Government has just passed a law making it illegal to loan money to serving members and their families at more than 36%. Most payday loan stores charge more than ten times that much, giving you $500 for a $575 cheque. That's $150 a month in interest if you can't pay it off.

31. **Pay down payday loans in steps:** If you do have payday loans, don't try to break yourself by going cold turkey. Most people who use these services can't afford to pay all the money back on one paycheque. Instead, write a slightly smaller cheque each time. If you borrow $500 one paycheque, try to limit yourself to $450 on the next one. It is slow, but you want to get out from under that nearly 400% annual interest any way you can.

32. **Lenders who advertise for bad risks have higher rates:** It is simple economics, people with bad credit are more likely to default, so lenders have to charge more interest to make up for the money from the loans that won't get paid back. So be aware that if you are buying a car from someone who says anyone who has a job has credit you will be paying more than you would otherwise.

33. **Don't get too many credit cards:** Getting more credit cards is a sure-fire way to get further into the debt trap. If one lender will give you $3500 in

credit based on your income, and you get the same from another lender you know have the potential for $7000 in consumer debt, an amount neither company would have extended. Multiple credit cards sound like a good way to get more credit, but what they really are is a way to make more interest payments.

34. **Deals that seem like an easy way out of debt usually aren't:** This one should be self-evident; businesses are rarely in business to enrich anyone other than their stockholders. The typical move is to offer to convert your consumer debt to a loan against your home equity. While it sounds good in principle, it not only frees up your credit cards to generate more debt (and more interest payments) but also gives the new creditor a lien on your house. Be careful when considering these deals.

35. **Don't co-sign for anyone:** It is simple enough; anyone who wants you to co-sign for them has worse credit than you do. In fact they have usually got a history of not paying loans back, and that means if you co-sign you are the one who is going to be paying it back. One co-signing agreement can cost you all the credit you have worked so hard to build up.

36. **Keep friendship separate from finances:** Nothing comes between friends faster than money and if you do lend a friend a large sum of money and they can't pay it back, you rarely have any recourse. This does not mean don't spot a

friend $10 towards pizza, but never lend a friend anything that you can't afford to lose. They will probably pay you back $10, and if they don't it won't break you.

37. **Don't take extra money when you go out:** If you are going out for the evening, don't take any more money than you plan on spending, because chances are you will spend everything you take with you. Once people start drinking, they tend to forget what else the money they have is supposed to be used for. Do yourself a favour and leave the grocery money at home.

38. **Don't take your bank card when you go out:** This is even more dangerous than taking extra money. Having the bank card means you can spend all the money you have, at least up to the daily withdrawal limit, and that's often enough to really wreck your budget. Now it is not something that will happen every time someone goes out. But it can happen and this is one of those cases where the cost is high enough that even a small risk is not worth taking.

39. **Budget for emergencies:** You will have expenses you did not think of when you made up your budget. Car repairs, something for the kids, suddenly discovering you need the septic tank pumped; something will always come up. The only way to deal with it is to expect it, and once you expect it, make sure you have money put aside to cover it. It may not be possible to have

enough to cover everything, but even having half the money set aside can help.

40. **Save something, no matter how little:** Saving is a lot like budgeting for emergencies, but with one major difference. You are expecting to spend your emergency budget, you just don't know when. Your savings are there to cover something like retirement, a down payment on a house, or some other future expenditure. It is money you don't expect to spend this year on anything. If you find yourself dipping into your savings every month, you are not saving and you need to re-evaluate your budget.

41. **Use multiple bank accounts:** It is really hard to manage your money if you keep it all in one account. A good plan is to have one account for saving, one for your day to day spending, and one for your bills. If you can possibly manage it, set the savings account up so you can't withdraw money with your bank card. Use the bill account for writing cheques, and also for any automatic withdrawals you have set up. Then the third account is the one you use for things like buying gas and groceries. This way any withdrawals you make won't come out of the money you have set aside for bills. It is all about taking control of your money and making it hard to make mistakes.

42. **Manage your money online:** Online banking is something else you should consider seriously. It lets you see what is happening with your money in real time, and also transfer money from one

account to another. If you can set it up for online bill payments and direct deposit, so much the better; as soon as your money comes in you pay your bills, move money over to savings and put the rest where you can get at it. You can also download your records to an accounting program as well which will save you time when you do your taxes.

43. **Save your receipts:** Keep your receipts for every major purchase or payment; you never know when they may come in handy. It is a lot easier to convince a credit reporting agency that you really did pay off that bill if you can fax them the receipt from the creditor proving they have received payment.

44. **Consider Layaway:** If you really need to buy something expensive and either you do not have credit or do not want to pay high interest rates, look into buying something on layaway. Yes you have to wait for what you are buying, but layaway is usually both more flexible and cheaper than buying something on credit, especially if the alternative is something like rent-to-own.

45. **Check local laws:** Different places have different laws, and some of those laws can come back to bite you if you are not careful. Some jurisdictions charge property taxes on vehicles, and can take your car if you don't pay. They may also impose a license fee, which usually has to be paid first, before they will accept money for the

taxes. These are small debts that can have a big impact if you do not pay them on time.

46. **Watch for hidden fees:** This could also be written as read the fine print, but either way it is important. Some agreements may have additional charges tacked on in the fine print, whether for paying the debt off early or for specific methods of payment. One company may outsource online bill payments to a third party who charges you to take your payment. These charges may be small, but taken together they can add up. Don't make a payment unless you know exactly where and how the money will be applied.

47. **Get overdraft on your bank account if you can:** One form of credit that is good to have is overdraft protection, though it is important not to use it unless you have to, like any other form of credit. The big advantage of overdraft is that it can prevent the bounced cheque cascade which can cost hundreds of dollars if one's not careful. Most banks only charge a nominal fee, in many cases only on months when you use it.

48. **Don't write cheques before the money comes in:** This one should be common sense but for too many people it's not. It is a game where the stakes are rarely worth the price. If the money doesn't come in on time the cheques may bounce. The problem is that not only do bounced checks cost you lots in fees, but they also affect your credit rating. The only way to get a perfect credit rating is to never bounce a cheque.

49. **Watch out for cascading bounce fees:** The world being the way it is, if you write several small cheques and one large cheque, and it turns out you do not have quite enough money to cover them, the first check to go through will always be the largest cheque, and it will make all the others bounce, even if the others were written first. Always make sure your account can cover every cheque you write or they will hit the bank in the most painful way possible. Banks make money on fees; expect them to maximize their income.

50. **Only one person can be in charge of the money:** This one's fairly simple, but easy to get caught on. A sure fire way to bounce a cheque is for one spouse to withdraw money the other was counting on to cover a cheque. The only way to prevent it is to make sure that one person is in charge of the money, and the other does not take money out beyond a certain point without checking with the first. It is just another way of keeping control of your money. It does not matter which spouse has control, only that one does and they both work together. Also, this does not mean one gives the other an allowance or makes all the financial decisions. It only means that once the decisions have been made, one person is keeping an eye on things.

51. **Don't max out your credit cards:** If you have to carry a balance on your credit card, always leave a cushion rather than maxing it out. That way your fees and interest charges are less likely to push your card over the limit and into penalty

territory. Those are charges that do nothing for you but lock out your card and drain your bank account. You don't want to go there if you can afford it.

52. **Pay the card off in full every month:** If at all possible, it is a good idea to pay your card off completely every month so that you can avoid paying interest. Many cards don't charge a cent in interest if you don't carry a balance; that can make a no annual fee credit card effectively free. Remember, interest is the enemy. Always arrange things to keep interest as low as possible.

53. **Close out credit accounts you no longer use:** This one's good if you are either building credit for the first time or rebuilding it. Quite often you may start with a higher interest credit card and then later on get a lower interest one from a different company. If you do, close the first one. Once you have got a major credit card there is no reason to keep that secured card or department store card you rarely use around. Close them down and control your bills.

54. **Look out for ATM fees:** Using an ATM other than your own banks can get you coming and going. Some of them charge additional withdrawal fees in addition to what your bank charges for using someone else's bank machine. If you have to use one of these machines, try to use it for larger withdrawals rather than smaller ones. With fees on both ends a $20 withdrawal can cost as much as $23 or more. But, since the

fees are fixed, getting $60 for $63 is a much better deal.

55. **Know what you need:** Also, know what you want rather than need. A big part of budgeting is separating luxuries from necessities and focusing on buying the necessities over the luxuries. If you spend too much on what you want you won't have enough for the things you actually need. Always prioritize your needs before your wants.

56. **Don't use credit card cash advances:** While credit cards often give you a break on interest if you pay them off before the end of the month, the interest clock starts ticking the moment you take a cash advance. Add in the possibility of ATM fees and cash advances become prohibitively expensive.

57. **Know when to buy cheap and when to buy quality:** Most of the time spending extra to get quality products is a good idea. A $60 pair of shoes will often not only fit better but last more than four times as long as a $15 pair of shoes. This is true 90% of the time, but if it's for something you are only going to use once, you are probably better off getting the cheap pair. If it is essentially disposable, go for the cheap option.

58. **Avoid buying on impulse:** Impulse buying is great fun, you see something and you have to have it immediately. Unfortunately sometimes it is not what you thought it was, or it's available for half the price somewhere else. If you really want

something take the time to find it elsewhere and see how you're going to fit it into your budget. It is all about keeping control of your money and getting the most value for each dollar.

59. **Pay off debt before increasing savings:** If you have got a windfall of a thousand dollars, you are better off in the long term to use it to pay down your debt rather than to put it into savings. If that is credit card debt you are carrying, paying down thousand dollars can save you two or three hundred dollars in interest alone over the course of a year. Paying off the debt early makes the money work harder for you.

60. **Do what you can yourself:** It always costs more to have someone else do something for you than to do it yourself. Learn to change your own oil if you don't already know. Know how to do basic repairs around the house. The more things you can do yourself the less you have to pay someone else to do, which will make your money go further and let you apply more of it to paying down your debt.

61. **Learn to barter:** Just as you can save money by doing things yourself, you can also save money by doing things for neighbours, especially if they have skills or tools you lack. Maybe you can fix the neighbour's computer and they can work on your car? It doesn't really matter which skills you have so long as you can help each other and save both of you some money.

62. **Consider a second job:** It may be obvious, but if you need more money, one option is to do more work. Get a second job and use all the money to pay off debts. If you have the skills look online for work, there are a number of sites which let you apply for freelance work that you can do around your regular schedule.

63. **Maintenance is cheaper than repairs:** Regular oil changes, just to use one example, are much cheaper than engine work, so it makes sense to budget for regular maintenance. I know there's a tendency not to want to spend money when you are on a tight budget, but paying for regular maintenance costs less money in the long run, and you pay on your schedule, not whenever the vehicle breaks down. Effective debt reduction only works when you are in control of your money, and maintenance helps keep you in control.

64. **Payroll deductions are your friends:** If you are working on reducing your debt, see if you can get your payments taken directly off your regular paycheque. Not only does this guarantee that those bills get paid, which is a good thing, but you will be surprised how quickly you adjust to the change in your regular take-home. It is all about making it easier to pay down your debts and easier to stick with the plan.

65. **Have them deduct more for tax:** If you can get your employer to deduct a little extra money from each check, not a lot just even five or ten dollars it

is worth doing. It provides insurance in case you are right on the edge between getting a return and having to pay, and if you do get another job the extra tax will help offset your earnings from that one. The other thing to remember is that doing this doesn't really cost you any money. Unless you owe the government money you will get it back on your tax return.

66. **See if your employer offers deals or special offers with other merchants**: The key to both controlling your debt and rebuilding your credit is to take control of all aspects of your finances and always get the most value for your money. One way to do that is check to see whether your employer gives deals on products from some of their business partners. It never hurts to look and if you were going to buy the product anyway, the savings will help.

67. **Budget for Christmas and Holidays throughout the year:** The holiday season can really put a crimp in your budget, especially if you have kids. No matter how hard you try it is almost impossible to keep your spending inside your regular monthly budget. So don't try. Put a little money aside every month and use that as a cushion. You know you are going to be spending the money anyway, so why not break it down over the course of the year. In the long run you will thank yourself and your kids can have a better holiday season that doesn't play hob with your carefully orchestrated payment plan.

68. **Divide all your payments up evenly for each cheque:** Most people use one cheque for rent and the other for bills. Since rent is usually higher, this means they have got spare money for half the month and things are tight the other half. There is a better option. Find out how much you are spending on bills and rent in total each month. Put half that amount into your bill-paying account each cheque. You get to pay all your bills on time and your finances stay on an even keel throughout the month.

69. **Don't rent to own:** Watch out for rent-to-own stores, they use sneaky tricks to hide the fact you are paying a lot more than the item's worth. They advertise the weekly price, but most people pay monthly, so that $19.99 a week comes to over $80 a month before they add taxes and insurance. Over a standard 24-month term that $600 stereo at the box store ends up costing you over $2000. It may help your credit if you pay on time every month, but the price of the loan isn't worth it.

70. **Remember free, and cheap, entertainment options**: Go for a walk in the park. Lots of towns offer various options that can help stretch your family's entertainment dollar/pounds. Take the kids to feed the ducks, maybe there is a free concert. You never know what you can find until you look, and every dollar/pounds you save is going to help.

71. **Apply for reduced lunches at school for your kids:** If you are working on either rebuilding

your credit or reducing debt, you probably don't have a lot of money. If you qualify you not only save by paying less for your children's lunches at school, but it will also lower your grocery bills. The less you have to spend on food, the easier it is to stick to your budget.

72. **Pay your parking tickets now:** Parking tickets add up. They often start low, but if you don't pay them in the first week or two, they start to increase, often dramatically. A ticket can be as little as $5 to $15 if you pay it in the first week or ten days, rising to $50 or $75 if it's not paid in a month. With rates like these there is a big benefit to paying your tickets before they become expensive.

73. **Cheque for Benefits:** Are you eligible for Food Stamps? What about WIC? Most importantly, do you know the answers to those questions? There are a number of programs that benefit low income families, and there is no reason you shouldn't be taking advantage of them. Take the time to go through the literature or websites and see what you can find. You may be eligible for benefits that will let you stretch your money that much further. Remember, the better you are living on your budget the easier your repayment plan will be.

74. **Take advantage of no-interest offers the smart way:** Every year you see them, ads for furniture saying no money down and no payments or interest for twelve months. They can be a great

deal, or if approached the wrong way they can be a terrible deal. If you do qualify, by all means take advantage. The trick to these is to ignore the no payment part. Start paying immediately, and pay as much as you can as fast as you can. If you get it paid off in that first year you didn't pay any interest, and that can save you hundreds of dollars on an expensive purchase.

75. **Buy Online:** Whenever possible, try not to buy before you have taken a look at prices online. While there is often a delay, and you do have to watch out for shipping costs, there are definite advantages to buying online. Unless the merchant is local, you normally won't have to pay sales tax, and depending on where you buy, you may be able to get free shipping.

76. **Small numbers add up:** When you are looking at your budget, one thing you need to pay attention to is how small expenses add up. Let's say you normally buy a large coffee and a muffin when you get to work and another coffee for the trip home. If the coffees cost $1.50 each, and the muffin $2 that adds up to $100 a month that you are spending. Coffee and a muffin do not sound like much, but every dollar you spend adds to the total.

77. **Don't sign up for things you don't need:** One of the quickest ways to drain your budget is with regular monthly fees. They can be anything from a gym membership to an online game subscription, but what they have in common is

they all come out of your bank account every month without fail. If you are not going to use the service every month, don't sign up for it. Either pay a little more for the months you do use it, or go without. If subscriptions cost $15 a month on a regular plan, or $18 a month if you buy one at a time, you only need to miss using it for one month to wipe out the savings on a six month subscription.

78. **Use transit whenever possible:** If you have access to public transit, use it. Yes you are tied to the schedule, but most major cities have regular service and expensive parking. In many cities you can get a month's pass on the transit system for what you pay in two weeks for parking. Add in the fact it does not put wear and tear on your car, or burn gas and you are saving money pretty quickly. The less you have to spend, the easier it is to stay out of debt.

79. **Lower your car insurance by not using it for work:** Insurers base their rates on a number of factors, one of which is how much you use the vehicle. You can usually insure a vehicle for pleasure use only, which is usually cheaper and will often let you take it to work about once a week for those occasions where you really need to.

80. **You can't rebuild credit without using credit:** It is one of those things, the way to get credit is to have a good credit report and you cannot get a good credit report without giving the credit

145

reporting agencies something to report. The trick is to use the credit wisely. Get a credit card and use it for something you are already doing like buying gas. Buy your gas with the card, pay it off each month and you will build a good credit history without costing yourself any money you aren't already spending.

81. **Once something goes to collections the original creditor doesn't have it:** It is no secret that most people don't like collection agencies. Some people so dislike them that they won't deal with them and insist on going to their original creditor. The problem with this approach is that creditors generally sell your debt to the collection agencies, and once they have done that they no longer have the debt. It takes work for them to get it back, and they won't normally do that unless they have to fix an error on their part. Once the bill goes to collection, you normally have to deal with the agency, not your original creditor.

82. **Watch out for Title loans:** They are always on TV, walk into the store, hand over your car title, and drive away with money. What you don't see is the interest rate, or that they take a set of keys as well as the title. A loan of $2000 can easily cost $400 a month in interest, and if you don't pay, they can (and will) come in the middle of the night and take your car. Yes it is a way to get money, but it is expensive, and you can lose your car if you have not budgeted for it. It is one debt you need to pay off quickly, and the only way to do that is to pay more than they ask each month.

All they ask for is the interest, because the longer you keep paying, the happier they are.

83. **Pawnshops are for buying, not borrowing:** Don't go to a pawnshop if you need money, they rarely give more than about 10-15% of the value of an item on loan, and like all such instant credit sources, interest rates are high. You are better off either selling the item to them, or only going there if there's something you want to buy. In too many cases pawning rather than selling an item means you are going to end up without the item or the money. It's not worth it.

84. **Pay extra on high interest loans:** The higher your interest rate, the better off you are making extra payments. The thing to remember is that if you make an additional payment, or a larger payment, all the extra money comes straight off the principal, it does not get applied to the interest. That means that even if you only make one additional payment, every payment you make after that one will put more towards reducing the debt rather than just servicing it.

85. **Time heals some wounds:** Most states have a statute of limitations on some debts. This does not mean the debt goes away, but what it does mean is that once a certain time has passed they are no longer able to sue you to recover the money. If someone comes to you with a very old debt, don't do anything until you have checked if it's covered by the statute.

147

86. **Rent is lost money:** Every dollar/pound you pay in rent is lost forever; every dollar/pound you pay on a mortgage becomes equity. Even if you do not have stellar credit, look into buying rather than renting. You may qualify for a first-time homeowner's loan, which can make the difference. However, like with anything else, you need to check and understand the interest rate. Some lenders use teaser interest rates in the short term, which increase to well above par after one or two years. Taking one of those home loans could put you into foreclosure, and that is a heavy blow to your credit.

87. **Saving a dollar is earning a dollar:** It does not matter how it got there, but every dollar you have in your bank account is worth the same at the end of the month. If you can save $50 by buying your groceries at the warehouse store instead of the supermarket it will have exactly the same effect on your finances as if you spent your usual amount at the grocery store and then someone handed you a cheque for $50. The other thing to remember is that this only counts when you are dealing with something you would have bought anyway, such as groceries or gasoline. Don't buy something you hadn't already budgeted for just because it's on sale.

88. **Look for the buyout on rent-to-own:** If you do have something from a rent-to-own store, start looking for the buyout as soon as you can. In most cases the buyout price is roughly equivalent to half the total of all your remaining payments,

so the sooner you can do the buyout, the more money you save. It is still going to be more expensive than buying from a box store would have been, but using the buyout can minimize your additional costs.

89. **Interest is never your friend:** Every dollar/pounds you pay in interest is like rent. It is money that is gone forever with nothing really left to show for it. Regardless of the circumstances you never want to pay a penny more in interest than you absolutely have to. Whenever possible pay as much principal as you can to reduce the portion of your payments that goes to interest.

90. **Debt settlement is not debt management:** Depending on your debt position, you may be able to make a settlement to clear some or all of your debts for less than face value. While it is a way to avoid bankruptcy, it is not without its costs. You not only have to get all your creditors to agree, but the difference between your outstanding debt and your settlement amount is classed as taxable income. Also, because all payments tend to go through the group negotiating the settlement, you are not paying the bills directly and that can show up as missed payments on your credit report.

91. **Debt management groups that charge fees work for you:** This is a simple example of follow the money. Companies work for the people who pay them. If you go to a fee-charging debt managing group they work for you and will often

try to get your debt reduced through a debt settlement plan as an alternative to bankruptcy.

92. **Free credit counsellors work for the creditors:** Most non-profit free credit counsellors are paid with a percentage of the money they collect for your creditors. Again, we follow the money. They have no incentive to try to reduce your total debt because that directly reduces their income. What they try to do is arrange payment plans at a lower interest rate so more of what you are paying actually goes toward the debt. Be aware of the differences when looking for debt assistance.

93. **Find out which method of paying your bills is cheapest:** Companies want to get their money, so most of them offer several ways to pay. There is cheque by phone, credit or debit card, mail them a check or even take cash down to the local office. Many places now offer online payment too. Take the time to see which fees apply to which method of payment. Is it cheaper to mail a check, or to use your credit card at their website? Take the time to find out and use that method. Any money you need to spend just to make a payment is a net loss. Whenever possible minimize or eliminate these charges.

94. **Quit smoking:** Cigarettes are expensive, and the costs are much higher than just what you pay for the carton. You also pay more in health insurance, and your income may drop due to lost wages due to smoking related health concerns. It

is also much easier to stick to a budget or anything else when you are in better health.

95. **You will have to pay those student loans:** When looking at debt repayment options and bankruptcy, pay particular attention to any student loans because most forms of debt relief do not apply to these debts. It is one of the reasons they are guaranteed, so students cannot graduate, declare bankruptcy and leave the government holding the bag for their education. There are ways to appeal, which can give relief for student loans, but they are difficult to qualify for.

96. **Pay your rent first, landlords look at credit reports:** Sad but true, if you have bad credit it is much harder to get a place to live. If you add eviction to a poor credit report it becomes doubly harder. Make sure to pay your rent on time every month. It is not worth the risk of eviction.

97. **Review your budget regularly:** Things change, and the budget that worked for you in June, may not work in December. You may have paid off one credit card, or perhaps you have a new bill. You need to make sure that your budget reflects your current needs and expenses. Keeping on top of your debts and rebuilding your credit requires that you know what is going on and be in control of your finances.

98. **Know the difference between secured and unsecured debt:** In its basic form, the difference is collateral. Unsecured debt is based on your

credit report and previous payment history. Secured debt is based on something the lender can take from you if you do not pay. Many forms of credit available to people with poor credit histories are secured debt, such as car title loans. If you have to delay a payment on one bill or another, consider whether the loan is secured or not as well as the interest rate.

99. **Get minimum payment insurance on your credit card:** It is a sad fact that most people in North America and UK today are living cheque to cheque, and with a high average debt load it is easy for a short period without employment to put someone in a situation it can take months or even years to recover from. This is why it pays to have payment insurance on your credit cards. If you do lose your job, the insurer will cover the minimum payments on your cards so your outstanding consumer debt does not go spiralling out of control.

100. **Always budget conservatively:** Round expenses up and income down. If you make $1275 a cheque, budget as if your income is $1250. Call your $52 dollar monthly phone bill $55 or $60 instead. Consistently following this principle will give you a little cushion to cover unexpected charges such as a pay-per-view movie that your son watched one night when you weren't home. It is another way of keeping control by expecting things won't go exactly as predicted. The closer you are to the edge, the more likely you are to go over. Adding in little

cushions by over-estimating expenses and under-estimating income keeps you just a little further from the edge.

101.   **Know the effect of credit applications:** Be aware of the fact that each time a potential lender checks your credit your credit score takes a slight hit whether you are approved or not. Because of this it is important to pick your applications carefully. You don't want to apply to every offer that comes in the mail, because each one you don't get will put you a little further behind. Wait until you have got a history of paying your bills on time before applying, and then apply to only one lender at a time and wait before you do another application.

Chapter 39: Conclusion

Bad credit mortgage lenders offer people with less than perfect scores on their credit reports the hope of owning their own homes. By offering higher interest higher fee sub-prime mortgages, bad credit mortgage lenders offer the chance for people with bad credit to own their own home.

Home ownership is part of the American dream. But, the average cost of a home is six to ten times an average person's salary depending on what part of the country you live in. The only chance of owning a home for an ordinary person is to take out a mortgage. If you have bad credit, it means going to bad credit mortgage lenders.

Many things can happen in people's lives to put them in a situation where they have bad credit. It may be the result of overextending yourself. It may be that you are bad about paying bills. You may have also had situations outside of your control like a major medical crisis or unexpected layoff. In any case, bad credit mortgage lenders give you a chance to achieve the American dream of homeownership.

Unfortunately, it is not as simple to get yourself out of a bad credit situation as it was to get into it. There are some things you can do immediately to improve your credit score, but other options take years of steady payments to improve the bottom line.

One thing you can do immediately is to obtain a free copy of your credit reports. Then, go through and see if there are any errors. If errors exist, report them immediately. The credit bureau has 30 days to confirm the debt. If they are unable to, then they must remove it from your records. This can help your credit score tremendously.

When you are thinking about buying a home, make sure you make all your payments on all of your bills on time for at least a year. This will improve your chances of getting a good rate on a loan.

But, when it comes to actually buying the home, you may find that you have no choice but to go to bad credit mortgage lenders. This will mean that you have a higher than average rate on your loan and you may also be required to pay extra points. The lender may also require that you take out insurance to secure the loan.

If you agree to these terms, you have a good chance of improving your credit over the next couple of years. That is because when you make payments on a home, it improves your credit score. After 24 months, consider refinancing the home because you should be able to get better rates after you have had the time to rebuild your credit.

Bad credit mortgage lenders offer subprime loans because the risk they take that you won't pay them back is outweighed by the higher rates and fees you pay. That's how bad credit mortgage lenders make their money.

Good Luck!